W9-AQW-101

Teaching
Students to Write

Argument

Essays That Define

▶ **Comparison/Contrast Essays**

Personal Narratives

Research Reports

Fictional Narratives

The Dynamics of Writing Instruction series

Peter Smagorinsky

Larry R. Johannessen

Elizabeth A. Kahn

Thomas M. McCann

with Angela Dean

LIBRARY
FRANKLIN PIERCE UNIVERSI
RINDGE, NH 03461

HEINEMANN

Portsmouth, NH

Heinemann
361 Hanover Street
Portsmouth, NH 03801–3912
www.heinemann.com

Offices and agents throughout the world

© 2012 by Peter Smagorinsky, Elizabeth A. Kahn, and Thomas M. McCann

All rights reserved. No part of this book may be reproduced in any form
or by any electronic or mechanical means, including information storage
and retrieval systems, without permission in writing from the publisher,
except by a reviewer, who may quote brief passages in a review.

"Dedicated to Teachers" is a trademark of Greenwood Publishing Group, Inc.

Library of Congress Cataloging-in-Publication Data
Teaching students to write comparison/contrast essays / Peter
Smagorinsky . . . [et al.].
ISBN-13: 978-0-325-03398-3
ISBN-10: 0-325-03398-6
Cataloging-in-Publication data is on file at the Library of Congress.

Editor: Anita Gildea *and* Lisa Luedeke
Development editor: Alan Huisman
Production: Sonja S. Chapman
Cover design: Monica Ann Crigler
Typesetter: Valerie Levy / Drawing Board Studios
Manufacturing: Steve Bernier

Printed in the United States of America on acid-free paper

16 15 14 13 12 PAH 2 3 4 5

CONTENTS

Preface

Despite all the attention that writing instruction received during the final decades of the twentieth century, the teaching of writing in middle and high schools remains, at best, uneven. National Writing Project sites have conducted countless summer institutes, and new books about teaching writing appear routinely in publishers' catalogues. Yet assessments continue to find that students' writing is less accomplished than teachers might hope. Undoubtedly, the assessments themselves are not what they ought to be (Hillocks 2002). But even those with relatively good reputations, such as the National Assessment of Educational Progress, find that students in the United States are not writing as well as many people expect them to. What's going on here? And will yet another book about teaching writing make a difference?

We have written this series of small books in the hope that they will provide alternatives for teachers who are dissatisfied with teaching five-paragraph themes, traditional grammar lessons, and other form-driven writing approaches. This book employs what we call *structured process*, an approach developed by George Hillocks during his years as a middle school English teacher in Euclid, Ohio, during the 1960s. Hillocks and his students have researched this method and found it highly effective (Hillocks, Kahn, and Johannessen 1983; Smith 1989; Smagorinsky 1991; Lee 1993). In a comprehensive research review, Hillocks (1986) found that over a twenty-year period, structured process writing instruction provided greater gains for student writers than did any other method of teaching writing.

We have spent a collective 120–plus years using structured process instruction in our high school English classes. We do not claim to have discovered the one best way to teach writing; rather, our goal is to explain in detail a method that we all found successful in our teaching. We hope you find this book useful and that your teaching benefits from reading and using the entire series.

How to Get the Most Out of This Book and This Series

The six books in this series help middle and high school teachers teach writing using a structured process approach, a method based on sound theory and research. Each book follows a similar format, focusing on a different type of writing: comparison/contrast essays (the focus of this volume), personal narrative, fictional narrative, essays that define, argument, and research reports. Although there are some general writing processes that apply to all types of writing, different kinds of writing require unique strategies. Therefore, the instructional activities in each book are tailored to that specific kind of writing.

The books show you how to design and orchestrate activities within an interactive and collaborative environment in which your students themselves experiment with ideas, debate these ideas with their peers, decide what and how to write, determine how to assess the quality of their writing, and discuss their work as a group. They include classroom-tested activities, detailed lesson sequences, and supporting handouts. The instruction is detailed enough to use as a daily lesson plan but general enough that you can modify it to accommodate you own curriculum and the specific needs of your students.

Most writing instruction emphasizes form. With a structured process approach, students first learn the thinking processes and strategies at the heart of a specific kind of writing, then consider form. This approach also recognizes that students write best when they want to communicate something that matters to them. The books show you how to introduce issues, dilemmas, and scenarios that capture students' interest and invoke the critical and creative thinking necessary to write powerfully and effectively. Samples of student writing are included; they illustrate students' learning and can also be used as instructional material for students to critique.

You may incorporate these books into a multiyear English language arts program, perhaps starting with personal narratives and fictional narratives in the earlier grades and moving to arguments, comparison/contrast essays, essays that define, and research reports in later grades. Alternatively, all six books in the series could constitute a yearlong writing course. Another option is to repeat modified sequences from one book at sequential grade levels, so students deal with that particular form at increasing degrees of complexity.

Although many of the activities and teaching strategies in these books can be used in isolation, they are most effective when included within a sequence of instruction in which students participate in increasingly challenging activities designed to help them become independent writers.

What's in This Book?

A brief introduction explains why we believe it's important to teach students to do the kind of thinking and writing required when one compares and contrasts. Chapters 1 and 2 demonstrate *how* to teach students to write comparison/contrast essays using structured process instruction; in them we describe classroom teaching strategies, provide a sequence of activities and handouts, and show examples of student work. Chapter 3 explains the structured process approach to teaching writing and its two main tenets, *environmental teaching* and *inquiry instruction*. This will help you understand why we designed the instruction modeled in this book the way we did; it will also help you design your own units of instruction in the future.

Why Teach Students to Write Comparison/Contrast Essays?

Comparing and contrasting is part of the daily thinking we go through when making choices. Do I have a doughnut for breakfast or a bowl of whole-grain cereal? On my way to work, when I see an accident up ahead on the superhighway, do I stay on the road or take the next exit in order to avoid the traffic jam? Once at school, do I start the day by grading papers, filling out paperwork, or heading to the lounge for coffee and conversation?

Each of these mundane decisions involves a process, however quickly it plays out. No matter how simple the choice, we usually make it in the context of its advantages in contrast with other choices. Doughnuts are yummy and easy and I can eat one on the fly; cereal is healthier but requires a bowl and spoon and milk and maybe a banana and I can't eat it while driving. A quick look at the clock and the decision's made.

Other types of thinking are more complex: which car to buy, which candidate to vote for, which job to take, among many others. Usually these decisions are made with a lot more deliberation and research.

Educators recognize the fundamental nature of the comparing/contrasting process, including it among the essential curricular modes to be taught and assessed. In vocational classes, students might choose which ensemble to wear for a job interview, which of several job avenues to pursue, or which brand of oil works best in a particular vehicle. Students in English classes might compare and contrast authors' styles, the value systems of different philosophical movements, or the themes explored by writers from different geographic regions. In the social studies curriculum, students compare and contrast the process and consequences of different economic

1

systems, the effectiveness of different leaders, or the perspectives behind different narratives capturing the same event. In science classes students can compare and contrast the differences among various kinds of butterflies, the makeup of different kinds of clouds and how they interact with other atmospheric elements, or the consequences for the environment of chemical and organic fertilizers and herbicides. The possibilities for applying these processes in school are legion, as they are in decisions that lead to a happy life in general.

Teaching students the intellectual and social processes involved in comparing and contrasting and the rhetorical features of this type of writing is one way to make school writing relevant, useful, and academically defensible. This book provides two illustrations of how to put the principles of a structured process approach into practice. Chapter 1 outlines how to teach comparison/contrast essays as a stand-alone type of writing—that is, without linking the writing to the rest of the curriculum. Chapter 2 uses a comparison/contrast essay as the central text in a unit on point of view (see www.coe .uga.edu/~smago/VirtualLibrary/Unit_Outlines.htm#PointOfView).

Preparing students to write well-developed, thoughtful comparison/contrast essays is time-consuming for both you and your students. The detailed, systematic lesson sequences in this book help students learn the necessary thinking and writing procedures. They will, we hope, also give you ideas for designing instruction using a structured process approach in other areas of your teaching.

Teaching Comparison/ Contrast Essays as Stand-Alone Writing

Life presents many choices. Which candidate do we support for president? Which Wimbledon finalist do we root for? How do we get to work, in a car or on a bicycle? Where shall we dine out tonight, Nuevo Leon or Señor Sol?

Young people make choices all the time. They vote for candidates for school offices and homecoming courts. They choose classes to take, video games to play, social activities to pursue, a career path to investigate, a college to attend. These choices often involve comparing and contrasting the available options. Comparing and contrasting two or more possibilities is a central facet of living in a world that offers seemingly unlimited choices. It makes sense, then, to include comparison/contrast essays in the writing curriculum.

Comparison/contrast instruction often jumps in at the deep end: students' first assignment is to write an essay comparing Faulkner with Hemingway, Realism with Naturalism, Lear with Macbeth, Iraq with Vietnam, or other complex pairings. We suggest instead starting with something more familiar and accessible so that students develop procedures before taking on topics that require more investigation and greater stretches in thinking.

Task Analysis

The way we decide between two Presidential candidates is a good starting point for helping students make similar kinds of choices. First, we need to _identify the points of comparison and contrast_—the issues on which we will compare and contrast the candidates. Figure 1–1 illustrates one possible way of placing the candidates' positions side by side. (Of course, a presidential race involves far more issues than those outlined.) With the points of comparison and contrast established, we then _characterize each candidate_ relative to each point.

Figure 1–1. Comparing and Contrasting Presidential Candidates

ISSUE	SMITH	JONES
Abortion	• Opposes abortion rights. • Has voted for abortion restrictions permissible under Roe v. Wade and would seek to overturn a guarantee of abortion rights. • Would not seek constitutional amendment to ban abortion.	• Favors abortion rights.
Death Penalty	• Supports expansion of the federal death penalty and limits on appeals.	• Supports death penalty for crimes for which the "community is justified in expressing the full measure of its outrage." • Supports videotaping interrogations and confessions in capital cases to minimize the possibility of wrongful convictions.
Education	• Favors parental choice of schools, such as vouchers for private schools and the right of parents to choose home schooling.	• Would encourage but not require universal prekindergarten programs, expand teacher mentoring programs, and reward teachers with higher pay not tied to standardized test scores. • Would change the national standardized testing program "so that we're not just teaching to a test and crowding out programs like art and music." • Favors a tax credit to pay up to $4,000 of college expenses for students who perform 100 hours of community service a year.

Figure 1–1. Comparing and Contrasting Presidential Candidates (*continued*)

Global Warming	• Favors tougher fuel efficiency and laws that would cut greenhouse gas emissions by 60 percent by 2050. • Supports more nuclear power.	• Favors tougher fuel efficiency and laws that would cut greenhouse gas emissions by 60 percent by 2050. • Supports more nuclear power. • Proposes a ten-year, $150 billion program to produce climate-friendly energy supplies.
Gun Control	• Opposes ban on assault-type weapons but favors requiring background checks at gun shows. • Would protect gun manufacturers and dealers from civil suits. Opposes gun control.	• Believes gun manufacturers and dealers should be open to lawsuits. • Supports a ban on all forms of semiautomatic weapons and tighter restrictions on firearms.
Health Care	• Opposes universal coverage. • Proposes a $2,500 refundable tax credit for individuals and $5,000 for families to make health insurance more affordable.	• Seeks universal coverage by requiring employers to share costs of insuring workers. • Would raise taxes on wealthiest families to finance the program.
Immigration	• Supports border fence. • Wants to allow illegal immigrants to stay in the U.S., work, and apply to become legal residents after they learn English, pay fines and back taxes, and clear a background check.	• Supports border fence. • Wants to offer legal status to illegal immigrants subject to conditions, including learning English and paying back taxes and fines.
The War	• Opposes scheduling a troop withdrawal because he believes "the surge" is working. • Supported the original invasion but criticized the manner in which administration went about it. • Supports troop increases and the construction of bases for permanent U.S. occupancy.	• Opposed war at start, opposed troop increase later. • Proposes to withdraw all combat troops within a year of being elected.

However, people may feel that one issue is more important than another or perhaps all others. For many people, the decision about the war overrides all the other considerations; their choice of candidate is thus clear and unambiguous. People concerned about global warming or immigration, areas in which the candidates appear to have rather similar policies, will need to pay greater attention to other issues. In order to make a good decision, then, voters need to *create priorities* about which issues matter most and rank them from most to least important. Doing so often requires *making a value judgment*, such as "Smith's position on gun control allows for an armed citizenry, which will deter crime," or "Jones' position on gun control will reduce the overall availability of guns, which will deter crime." With either position viable, voters need to make an evidence-based choice.

Here is a set of procedures people might use to compare and contrast two potential choices:

- Identify the points of comparison and contrast.

- Characterize each choice in terms of the points of comparison and contrast.

- Create priorities among the points of comparison and contrast.

- Compare and contrast the two choices.

- Make a value judgment.

These procedures might or might not be linear. For instance, creating priorities might come first: a voter might see candidates' positions on abortion to be so important at the outset that everything else falls into line behind it. Then again, the process of comparing and contrasting might elevate the importance of other issues and even cause one to change one's initial value judgments.

In teaching students comparison and contrast strategies, you next design a set of comparison activities that will enable students to write essays explaining the value of each option. Planning such instruction involves several considerations. One decision concerns the topics to be compared and contrasted. Ultimately, students will select their own topics. But for whole-class instruction in the procedures, areas of common interest seem appropriate. Asking students for topics related to their own social worlds is a good way to start.

Stage 1. Gateway Activity: Analyze Similarities and Differences

EPISODE 1.1. Ask students to suggest two relatively similar things to compare and contrast: two fast-food restaurants, two musicians who perform the same genre, two athletes who play the same position, two celebrities who are in the headlines, or any other pair of similar people, places, or things. (Tell them not to pick two people from your school, which will keep you out of hot water.)

For illustrative purposes, assume students decide to compare and contrast how two radio stations are similar and different. They observe that while both stations play a core of mainstream rock, they are different in a number of ways: WXYZ plays more urban and hip-hop music, while WABC plays more country and western; WXYZ has more political features, while WABC's disc jockeys talk more about celebrities; WXYZ pairs men with women for their drive-time broadcasts, while WABC's disc jockeys behave like frat boys; WXYZ has interviews with musicians while WABC has an afternoon sports show.

After recording the comments, ask students to categorize the points they have made. Their observations could be classified according to the genres of music played, the kinds of disc jockeys employed, and the nonmusical features of the programming. Create a chart similar to the graphic used for comparing political candidates in Figure 1–1: list the categories for comparison and contrast in the left column and the examples for the two radio stations in the next two columns. Explain that students have *identified the points of comparison and contrast* between the two stations and *characterized each station* according to the points of comparison and contrast.

Ask whether any of these categories are more important than the others. One student may find the type of music is paramount; another may feel the quality of the banter between disc jockeys rules; still another may insist the celebrity features trump all. Identify this additional feature of comparing and contrasting: *creating priorities among the points of comparison and contrast* in order to refine the task and personalize the process.

EPISODE 1.2. In small groups have students:

- Compare and contrast the two stations in relation to each point of comparison and contrast.

- Make a value judgment about which of the two stations they prefer.

When they finish, have them report back to their classmates, who have the opportunity to raise questions about each group's thinking. Students are therefore prompted to think critically about their decisions and are responsible for communicating their ideas and reactions, areas in which teachers usually tend to dominate classrooms (see Marshall et al. 1995 and Nystrand 1997). This shift puts students in greater control of their own learning.

Thus far, students have done a lot more talking than writing. Talking about the issues becomes the basis for their later writing: the students experience the processes they will employ and get feedback on their thinking in real time. The writing will potentially yield new insights, but discussion at this early stage is a powerful way for students to learn thinking processes they can later apply to similar tasks.

Stage 2. Apply Comparison/Contrast Procedures to a New Task

Moving toward independence, students now compare and contrast elements they have chosen themselves—and with which they are familiar without needing to conduct additional research—thus enhancing their ability to be successful. Students might compare a Ford pickup with a Chevrolet pickup, the soccer player Ronaldo with his fellow Brazilian Ronaldinho, one line of cosmetics with another, the *Dragon Ball* manga series to the *Dragonquest* manga series, one baba ghanoush recipe with another, Sunnis with Shiites, Cantonese eggrolls with Philippine eggrolls, Jimmy Fallon with Conan O'Brien—the possibilities are endless.

EPISODE 2.1. Have students, in small groups, select two places, people, things, or events to compare and contrast. They should pick things they know a lot about so they'll be well informed about them. Suggest that they pick any school-appropriate pair of items that are more or less similar: two pizza parlors, two musicians in the same genre, two cars in the same vehicle class, two stores of the same type, and so on. (Again, exclude people from your school.) As a reminder, project a list of the steps in the process:

- Identify the points of comparison and contrast between the two items.

- Characterize each item in relation to the points of comparison and contrast.

- Create priorities among the points of comparison and contrast.

- Compare and contrast the two items.

- Make a value judgment.

Stress that this list is not a strict sequence; students just need to be sure to include each of these procedures somewhere along the way. Tell them they have thirty minutes. (If there is time and the technology is available, students can supplement their own knowledge with information from the Internet or other sources.)

In a class in which Angele Dean presented this lesson, a group of boys compared two basketball players, Kobe Bryant and Tracy McGrady: both went straight from high school to professional basketball, are roughly the same height, and play the same position. They compared and contrasted the two players' physical features, statistics, and accomplishments and concluded that Kobe Bryant is a better player than Tracy McGrady. The points of comparison they identified are listed in Figure 1–2.

EPISODE 2.2.   After the groups complete their comparison/contrast, have each group report back to the class (using presentation software if they wish). Let classmates question and critique their work, and have the groups either defend or revise their conclusion. Reflecting on their process and sharing these reflections makes students consciously aware of the procedures they are learning.

Figure 1–2. Points of Comparison/Contrast: Kobe Bryant vs. Tracy McGrady

KOBE BRYANT	TRACY McGRADY
African American	African American
MVP 2008	Houston Rockets
Los Angeles Lakers	Adidas
	Rookie of the year
Nike Lowtops	Captain
Hops, jumps over car	
	15 pts per game
Fade-away	6'8"
	Straight from N.C. private high school
Captain	11 yrs pro
6'7"	223 lbs
27.1 pts per game	30 yrs old
Ball hog/fast	Won community award
Straight from Lower Merion HS	Player in Olympics
12 yrs pro	
205 lbs	
National high school player of the year	
Youngest player in NBA	
Player in Olympics	

Stage 3. Generate Task-Specific Evaluative Criteria

One way to help students develop evaluative standards is for them to consider the qualities of a set of comparison/contrast essays and generate their own criteria based on their assessments.

EPISODE 3.1. Present this assignment:

Read the three essays I've given you, which compare and contrast two breakfast cereals. Then, in a small group, decide which essay is best, which is second best, and which is third best. Your small group will represent one of the following types of readers:

- readers evaluating the state writing test
- high school English teachers
- hungry teenagers who can't decide what to eat for breakfast
- representatives from the manufacturers of the cereal companies
- parents who must be convinced which cereal to buy for their teenagers

- lumberjacks who are unfamiliar with the brands and can only buy one box of cereal before a big day of chopping down trees.

As you work, take notes, because you will need to explain the reasons behind your ranking.

The three essays (A, B, and C) are shown below. Each deliberately has some positive qualities and some problems. Students also have to tease out whether the readers they represent would value organization over insight, correct standard English over a strong voice, and so on.

Essay A

In this essay I will compare two cereals that are very similar, Oat Rings and Fruit Hoops. Both have many similarities. Each one is a breakfast cereal. Each one is shaped like a little tire. Each one is yummy. But, in fact, they are also very different. I will next explain why.

Oat Rings is made by the Giant Foods Corporation in the USA, which is ironic because each oat ring is in fact quite small. Fruit Hoops is made by the Kloggs company, which is also ironic because it is a high-fiber cereal. So that's one difference right there, even though they are also similar.

Both Oat Rings and Fruit Hoops have ingredients. But the ingredients are different. In Oat Rings you will find whole grain oats, modified corn starch, corn starch, sugar, salt, trisodium phosphate, calcium carbonate, monoglycerides, tocopherols, wheat starch, and annatto. On the other hand, in Fruit Hoops there is sugar, corn flour, wheat flour, oat flour, partially hydrogenated vegetable oil (one or more of: coconut, cottonseed, and soybean), salt, sodium ascorbate, ascorbic acid, natural orange, lemon, cherry, raspberry, blueberry, lime, other natural flavors, red #40, blue #2, yellow #6, zinc oxide, niacinamide, turmeric color, blue #1, annatto color bht (preservative), and folic acid. As you can see, the ingredients are different, and Fruit Hoops has many more ingredients.

There are other differences too. In Oat Rings you will find the daily minimum requirement of many important vitamins. You get 0% for vitamin A, 0% for Vitamin C, 4% for calcium, 35% for iron, 0% for vitamin D, 5% for thiamine, 3% for riboflavin, 5% for niacin, 15% for vitamin B-6, 10% for folate, 0% for vitamin B-12, 5% for pantothenate, 7% for phosphorus, 10% for magnesium, and 10% for zinc. You get even more of these things if you add milk. On the other hand, in Fruit Hoops you will find 4% for vitamin A, 7% for Vitamin C, 0% for calcium, 15% for iron, 10% for vitamin D, 4% for thiamine, 0% for riboflavin, 9% for niacin, 11% for vitamin B-6, 12% for folate, 0% for vitamin B-12, 15% for pantothenate, 6% for phosphorus, 9% for magnesium, and 18% for zinc. As is the case with Oat Rings, you get more of each one if you add milk. The only way in which they are the same is that both provide 0% of your daily vitamin B-12 needs, although that probably changes if you add milk.

In conclusion, Oat Rings and Fruit Hoops are both cereals that you can eat for breakfast or other meals, or snacks. Both are delicious. I recommend that you eat Fruit Hoops because with fruit it is healthier and the additional ingredients make it even healthier. And if you add milk, you will have a nutritious, delicious breakfast.

Essay B

Oat Rings and Fruit Hoops are both breakfast cereals they are similar and different in many ways. I will next tell you how. The flavor of the two is really different, Oat Rings, as the name suggests, is made mainly from oats and so has an oaty flavor. Its also lite on sugar and so you taste oats more than sweetness. Whereas Fruit Hoops first ingredient is sugar not flour and so its way sweet which many people like. Both are shaped exactly the same like a little bagel and they are equally crunchy as long as you dont add too much milk. Both are deciduous. Oat Rings are also healthier because its pretty much just oats in their and there healthy. Whereas Fruit Hoops needs color so it has got alot of fake colors like red #40, blue #2, yellow #6, turmeric color, blue #1, & annatto color bht whatever that is. Both serials come in many varieties Oat Rings comes in Honey Heaven Berry Bunches Yogurt Yummys Multigrain Crunchios Fruitios Frostios and Apple Raisin. Whereas Fruit Hoops comes in Marshmellow Hoops Low Sugar Hoops Big Bang Hoops with caffeine and Fruit Hoops flavored Toast-R Tarts. These choices give you plenty of variety expecially when you buy the variety pack. In conclusion I recommend that you eat Oat Rings instead of Fruit Hoops because they are healthier because they're first ingredient is oats not sugar and because they do not have fake colors to stimulate fruit colors. Just add milk and youll have an even healthier way to start your day.

Essay C

Many people begin their day with a nice bowl of cereal. Often they have to start the day by choosing between two kinds. Suppose you got up one day and were hungry and opened the cabinet and found one box of Oat Rings and one box of Fruit Hoops and had to make a choice. What would you do? I often solve problems like this by writing an essay comparing and contrasting the two things. So that is what I will do now. By the end of my essay I will convince you that the best way to start your day is with a delicious bowl of Fruit Hoops.

Both of these cereals are delicious and nutritious and are shaped like little donuts. Just reading the side of the box makes me want to get out a bowl and a spoon and some milk and dig in. For example Oat Rings is full of delicious oats which may lower cholesterol which is why it is certified by the American Heart Association. It also contains 14 vitamins & minerals, is low in fat, has less then 3 grams of fat in each serving, has 10% of the calcium you need for the day, has plenty of fiber, has only 1 gram of sugar, is a good source of iron, and may reduce the risk of heart disease as part of a heart-healthy diet. Fruit Hoops are also delicious but not because of oats, because of the sweet and fruity flavor. The very first ingredient in Fruit Hoops is sugar which means that there's more sugar in it than anything else. Mmmmmmmmm. Furthermore Fruit Hoops ingredients include many extra flavors including orange, lemon, cherry, raspberry, blueberry, lime, and other natural flavors. Because they are natural they are healthy and so good for you. Fruit Hoops also includes oats which are in Oat Rings and also corn and wheat, which gives them the triple whammy of nutrition. And the corn that they use contains traces of soybeans, which are especially healthy. As you can see both of these cereals are delicious and healthy because of their many totally excellent ingredients. So how do you choose between them.

I believe that Fruit Hoops provide the best breakfast to start the day because they have so many healthy ingredients and a nice sweet taste that gets rid of "morning breath" too. And the healthy amount of sugar gives you that extra energy you need to get you going in the morning, especially if you get Big Bang Hoops with Caffeine. And so in conclusion, my comparison and contrast of Oat Rings and Fruit Hoops proves that for a healthy, deliciously sweet breakfast that gets you going without morning breath, Fruit Hoops is the way to start your day.

Ask student groups to choose which audience they want to represent. Then, as a class, discuss what each particular group might look for in each essay:

1. State evaluators are likely to look first to mechanical aspects of the essay and whether spelling or grammar mistakes stand out; accuracy in details provided is also a consideration. These readers will probably look for a logical argument in which the writer stays on topic and maintains an organized presentation of ideas. (Since teachers will most likely have the same concerns, have one of the small group represent both viewpoints.)

2. Teens might be more concerned with descriptions of the cereals; they might want to be able to imagine what the cereal looks like and how it tastes.

3. Manufacturers probably want to know what aspects of the cereal they can use as selling points and how best to market their product; taste is important, as well as any other information they can use to create advertisements, persuade the consumers, and finally bring in profits.

4. Many parents will place nutrition and price first; they'll want to know how it might help or hurt their child nutritionally. Brand is also important. If they know and trust the brand, parents might purchase the cereal for their children.

5. The number of servings per box will no doubt be important to the lumberjacks, along with nutrition and how filling the cereal is. Price could also be significant, since lumberjacks work hard and don't want to waste money on unhealthy food. Lumberjacks probably want a cereal that helps them feel energized and ready for a long day at work.

In Angela's class, the members of the state evaluator/teacher group chose essay C as the strongest because it has a clear thesis, the opening and closing paragraphs are strong, it supports its argument with details, and it is more mechanically sound than the other essays. They felt that the essay isn't overly opinionated and flows well. They rated essay A next because it emphasizes comparing and contrasting equally and is persuasive. However, the mechanical aspects are not as strong as essay C's. They placed essay B last because its opinions and facts are not as thorough, and it doesn't seem to be aimed at an audience of this kind.

Both the teen group and the manufacturing group placed the essays in the same order. They ranked Essay B first because it emphasizes taste over factual information, and how the cereals taste is of greatest importance to the consumer (the teens) and the manufacturers (as a selling point). They ranked essay C next. The opinions and the description of the cereal it offers are important to both groups. Although the essay doesn't mention nutrition, neither group was concerned with the product's nutritional value. They placed essay A last because it focuses solely on facts and nutrition and therefore doesn't speak to these groups.

The parent group ranked the essays in the order A, B, C. Essay A addresses parents' concern for ingredients; essay B speaks to the nutritional value parents may worry about; and essay C only deals with taste, which Angela's students felt is not a significant concern for this audience.

The lumberjacks group preferred essay C, because their number one concern was how filling a cereal might be, given the kind of work they do. They ranked essay A second because it speaks to nutrition—lumberjacks don't want to put something without nutritional value in their bodies. They placed essay B last because it doesn't address how filling and nutritional the cereals are.

EPISODE 3.2. Have students generate *criteria* they believe should be applied to writing of this sort. Acknowledge differences in the readerships represented by the different groups and consider the extent to which writing quality has universal criteria or depends on the expectations of anticipated readers.

EPISODE 3.3. Have students, in small groups, reconsider their original criteria in light of their exchanges with other groups and use a template (available on web sources such as www.rubistar .com or www.learner.org/workshops/hswriting/interactives/rubric/) to construct a *rubric* by which their essays will be evaluated. This process helps students look beyond whatever bias exists in their original assumptions and move their thinking to a new and broader consideration of what is involved in a comparison and contrast of two items of a similar type.

EPISODE 3.4. Have each group report to the class, displaying their rubric as an overhead transparency or by some other means. Have students from other groups offer critiques that will prompt additional discussion of the assessment criteria, and help the class settle on a single rubric for grading the essays.

The group rubrics will probably range from four criteria to eight criteria. Ask students how they might feel receiving a rubric with many criteria or one with only four or five criteria. Show them a rubric with fifteen criteria, which they may find quite overwhelming. Students given such a long list might not bother to write—they'd feel they could never meet the standards and get a good grade. Discuss which criteria students feel have to stay and which can go.

Reiterate the requirements of a comparison/contrast essay: identifying two things that have similarities and differences, collecting details regarding each item, organizing the details into categories, ranking these categories in order of importance, and finally creating a value judgment. Help students see how these steps lead to the requirements of a comparison/contrast essay. The value judgment is linked to a strong thesis statement. The details provide support for the argument. Creating and ranking categories prompts the essay's organization and paragraph development.

Next, discuss evaluative rankings: numbers (four to one or one to four), usually linked to descriptors such as *advanced, proficient, basic,* or *needs improvement*. Write a list of descriptors on the board, and have the class whittle away at it, making their own unique list. Students should discuss the pros and cons of each descriptor and how they might feel as writers if their work were categorized that way.

Point out that the descriptors *needs improvement, weak,* and *unacceptable* may make them feel they have nothing to offer. If given a label like this on a writing assignment, they might not want to write any further. Discuss the important idea that we must look for what is present in the writing rather than focusing on what the writing lacks, thus nurturing reluctant writers rather than making them question their decision to take risks and make an effort. Have the students generate the categories by which they wish to have their work evaluated, linked to particular degrees of proficiency in the rubric.

Next discuss what the rubric should evaluate. Angela's students determined that organization should be the first requirement, because the essay needs to flow logically so that the reader can easily follow the writer's argument and supporting details; paragraph development can be part of this criterion. Details were the next criterion her students valued, because accurate information is necessary to support the overall argument and persuade the reader to see things from the writer's perspective. They combined audience and tone into one area, since one cannot consider audience without thinking about the tone of the piece. An audience isn't likely to respond to an argument presented in a supercilious or argumentative tone. Grammar, spelling, and punctuation were the last criterion they listed on the rubric. (An example of a final rubric is shown in Figure 1–3.)

At the end of the session, say, "Look back to our rubric. Is there anything your group might change in your essay, considering your audience? If so, make the changes or additions and provide a reason for your changes."

Figure 1–3. Example Rubric for a Comparison/Contrast Essay

	ADVANCED (4)	ACCOMPLISHED (3)	IMPROVING (2)	EMERGING (1)
Organization and Paragraph Development	Logical presentation of ideas; all parts contribute to a strong central idea; each paragraph always relates to the topic and presents details that allow the reader to understand the argument more completely; paragraphs flow seamlessly from one to the other.	Most ideas are connected; some parts contribute to the central idea; many paragraphs relate to the topic and often present convincing details; paragraphs flow seamlessly from one to the other.	Some ideas connected to each other; many parts don't contribute to the central idea; some paragraphs relate to the topic and present convincing details that support the argument; transitions between paragraphs are sometimes smooth.	Ideas have little connection to each other; there is no strong central idea; few or no paragraphs relate to the topic; transitions between paragraphs are awkward.
Details	Uses details that are always accurate, appropriate, and fully support the topic.	Uses details that are mostly accurate and typically support the topic.	Uses some details that are accurate; some details are not appropriate for the topic; details do not always support the topic.	Uses little or no detail to support and explain the topic.

Figure 1–3. Example Rubric for a Comparison/Contrast Essay (*continued*)

Audience and Tone	The writer has correctly identified the intended audience; writing shows a complete understanding of its expectations; tone matches the intent of the piece appropriately, enhancing a readers experience and understanding.	The writer has correctly identified the intended audience; writing shows that the writer is somewhat aware of its expectations; appropriate tone is consistently maintained throughout the piece.	The writer has an incomplete idea of the audience and its expectations; inconsistent tone or tone considered in some parts but not the entire essay.	The writer has not identified the audience; writing does not address a specific audience; tone is not appropriate for the topic or audience.
Grammar, Punctuation, Spelling	Uses completely appropriate grammar that helps readers understand meaning; no errors in punctuation; all words are spelled correctly, helping readers clearly understand the central idea.	Uses appropriate grammar that does not interfere with meaning; a few punctuation errors; most words are spelled correctly.	Grammar choices sometimes confuse readers; many or major errors in punctuation that sometimes confuse the reader; there are many spelling errors that sometimes make it hard for the reader to understand the central idea.	Grammar choices keep readers from understanding the piece; frequent and/or major errors in spelling that obscure meaning; there are frequent spelling errors that make it hard for the reader to understand the central idea.

For example, the group in Angela's class writing about Kobe Bryant and Tracy McGrady made the following elaborations:

Kobe is a better player than Tracy.

    I.   Kobe has better statistics.

        A.   For example, Kobe averages 27.1 points per game; McGrady averages 15 points per game.

    B.   Kobe and McGrady can both shoot 3s, but Kobe has a sick fade-away.

    C.   Kobe has 12 yrs in the NBA; McGrady has 11 yrs in the NBA.

  II. Kobe has more accomplishments than McGrady.

    A.   Kobe has been awarded the MVP, in 2008; McGrady hasn't.

    B.   They both played in 2008 Olympics.

    C.   They were both Rookie of the Year.

Their final outline based on these elaborations provided the following information:

Kobe Bryant vs. Tracy McGrady

Comparison/Contrast Essay

    TS: Topic Sentence
    D: Data
    W: Warrant
    CS: Concluding Statement

Introduction: In the NBA, there are many great teams. Over all there are two teams with incredible players. The Rockets and the Lakers. These two athletes are Kobe Bryant and Tracy McGrady. They have many skills that we will talk about.

Thesis: Kobe is a better player than Tracy.

Body Paragraph 1

(TS): Kobe is a better player statistically.

(D): Kobe averages 27.1 points per game; McGrady averages 15 points per game.

(W): This shows that Kobe is better on the court at shooting and makes up most of his team's points.

(W): This shows that Kobe is a bit of a ball-hog, but it's for the good of the team.

(D): Kobe and McGrady can both shoot 3's; but Kobe has a sick fade-away.

(W): They can both shoot 3's pretty good, but when they are blocked, Kobe can resort to his fade-away.

(W): Kobe is better, because he has more than one method to score and get more points. Plus, Kobe has a better style of shooting.

(D): Kobe has 12 yrs in the NBA; McGrady has 11 yrs in the NBA.

(W): They both have been around for a while, but Kobe has a bit more experience than T-Mac, which makes him better.

(W): But as we can tell, they are both seasoned veterans.

(CS): In conclusion, Kobe is a better player because he has more years, better shooting, more points than McGrady.

Body Paragraph 2

(TS): Kobe has more accomplishments than McGrady.

(D): Kobe has been awarded MVP, in 2008; McGrady hasn't.

(W): This shows that Kobe has been successful in 2008 and he got awarded for playing good.

(W): This shows that McGrady is playing good, but not as good as Kobe.

(D): They both played in 2008 Olympics.

(W): This shows that they both played really good in the '08 season and went to the Olympics.

(W): This shows that they have enough skill to impress the U.S. coach and earn a spot on the national team.

(D): Kobe also got high school player of the year and Mc-Grady didn't.

(D): They were both rookie of the year.

(W): This shows that they were talented coming into the pros and playing their best in their rookie year.

(CS): In conclusion, Kobe is a better athlete than T-Mac because he has earned more awards than McGrady.

Conclusion: In conclusion, to our information, you can clearly see that Kobe Bryant is a better player than Tracy McGrady. Stats show the advantage Kobe has over Tracy.

Stage 4. Write in Small Groups

Students, in the same small groups that generated the information, now attempt their first draft. Composing as a group, students learn how to put information into an appropriate form in a situation in which they can co-construct knowledge and receive continual feedback on their thinking (see Dale 1994).

EPISODE 4.1. Have each group specify the community of readers who will evaluate their essay, revising the class rubric as necessary. Here's the assignment:

In your small group, compose an essay in which you compare and contrast two school-appropriate people, places, things, or events of your choice. Remember the procedures we have used in our discussions thus far:

1. Make sure you compare and contrast two items that are generally similar yet different in ways you can identify and explain.

2. Before you begin writing:

   a. Identify the points of comparison and contrast between the two items.

   b. Characterize each item in relation to the points of comparison and contrast.

   c. Create priorities among the points of comparison and contrast.

   d.   Compare and contrast the two items.

   e.   Make a value judgment about the two items.

3.   Using the rubric you have prepared as your guide, compose an essay in which you present and support your comparison and contrast.

Circulate among the groups as they work, keeping the students on task and answering their questions. In Angela's class the group comparing Bryant and McGrady, writing for an audience of coaches, staff members, fans, youth, and teachers, produced the essay shown below.

Group Essay on Kobe Bryant vs. Tracy McGrady

In the NBA, there are many great teams. Over all, there are two teams with incredible players. The Rockets and the Lakers. These two athletes are Kobe Bryant and Tracy McGrady. They have many skills that we will talk about.

Kobe is a better player statistically. He averages 27.1 points per game, while McGrady averages 15 points per game. This shows that Kobe is better on the court at shooting and makes up most of this team's points. This also shows that Kobe is a bit of a ball-hog, but it's good for the team. Another detail is that both Kobe and McGrady can shoot 3's, but Kobe has a sick fade-away. This shows that Kobe can resort to his fade-away if he's blocked, but McGrady can't. This also shows that Kobe is better because he has more than one method to score. Kobe also has a better style of shooting. The last detail is that Kobe has 12 yrs in the NBA, while McGrady has 11 yrs in the NBA. This proves that Kobe is better because Kobe has more experience playing. Still, you can tell they are both seasoned veterans. In conclusion, Kobe is better statistically because he has more years playing, he has better shooting, and he averages more points than McGrady.

Kobe has more accomplishments than McGrady. Kobe has been awarded MVP, in 2008, and McGrady hasn't. This shows that Kobe has worked hard during the season and was awarded at the end. This also shows that McGrady has been playing good, but not as good as Kobe. Kobe played in the 2008

Olympics. This shows that Kobe is better because he played to his potential and was able to impress the coach of the United States team. They were both rookie of the year. This shows that they were talented coming into the pros and playing their best in their first year. Kobe also got a High School player of the year award and McGrady didn't. In conclusion, Kobe is a better athlete than T-mac because he has earned more awards than McGrady.

In conclusion, based on our information, you can clearly see that Kobe Bryant is a better player than Tracy McGrady. Stats show the advantage Kobe has over Tracy. Accomplishments, awards, and their number of years in the NBA also show that Kobe is better.

EPISODE 4.2.   When a group completes its essay, have the members present a written copy to a different group, who role-play being members of the intended audience and use the class rubric (as revised if necessary) to evaluate the essay and submit an assessment. Have each peer response group assign the essay a letter grade based on the rubric's rankings and explain in writing how the writers performed in relation to each assessment criteria.

EPISODE 4.3.   Ask the small groups to revise their essays. Then grade the essays, using the rubrics students have provided. Also ask students to write informal reflections on how they went about writing their essays. Examining their writing process enables students to name the processes they have developed so they may consciously apply them in the future.

Stage 5. Present a Language Lesson on Using Subordinating Conjunctions

Comparing and contrasting two things often involves sentences that include subordinating conjunctions—words such as *although* and *since* that qualify a statement. The exercise in Figure 1–4 helps students construct complex sentences (those including both an independent and a dependent clause) by using subordinating conjunctions.

Figure 1–4. Combining Sentences Using Subordinating Conjunctions

A subordinating conjunction connects two types of clauses:

- An independent clause (one that can stand on its own as a complete sentence).

- A dependent clause (one that cannot stand on its own and must be attached to an independent clause).

Common subordinating conjunctions include the following words:

after

although

as

because

before

how

if

once

since

than

that

though

till

until

when

where

whether

while

Here are some examples of these words acting as subordinating conjunctions. Note that either the independent or the dependent clause may come first in the sentence.

Until someone convinces me otherwise, I'll take Oat Rings over Fruit Hoops any day.

(*continues*)

Figure 1–4. Combining Sentences Using Subordinating Conjunctions (*continued*)

> I prefer Fruit Hoops over Oat Rings, *though* some days their sugary sweetness makes my teeth ache.
>
> *After* I eat dinner, I often eat a giant bowl of Oat Rings for dessert.
>
> Fruit Hoops-flavored Toast-R Tarts are delicious *because* they have so much extra sugar in them.

Connect the pairs of sentences below using one of the subordinating conjunctions listed above in order to form a complex sentence.

1. Some people prefer listening to the tenor saxophone.
   I would rather hear the soprano.

2. El Toro serves its chips hot and crisp.
   At Los Compadres the chips are served cold and soggy.

3. The Times New Roman font is a big favorite.
   I like Arial much better.

4. The Jack Russell Terrier is a very popular breed of dog.
   I find them to be rather nippy, yippy, and zippy.

5. Olson's Hardware Store carries many types of hex nuts.
   Generic Tools only has the standard sizes.

6. The red buckeye flowers early in the spring.
   White buckeyes flower in mid-summer.

7. Bill Cosby talks a lot about his family in his comedy.
   Eddie Izzard talks more about history.

8. Truck commercials seem targeted to tough guys.
   Minivan commercials are designed for family consumers.

9. Chinese egg rolls are filling and come in a wheat dough wrapper.
   Vietnamese egg rolls are wrapped in rice paper and are lighter.

10. In season one of *24*, Jack Bauer was married to Teri.
    In season two Jack's girlfriend was Kate Warner.

Stage 6. Write from Sources

Thus far students have been dealing with familiar topics and have been able to rely on their personal knowledge to provide the content for their essays. Now they begin working with less familiar, more complex topics that require consulting sources for information.

Nelson and Hayes (1988), investigating how college students approached writing from sources, found that weaker students went on fact-finding missions and then reproduced their sources' ideas verbatim. Stronger students found information that helped them argue a position and looked at the source material from an original perspective. Writers should not simply juxtapose pieces of information but use the information to draw an original and forceful conclusion.

In the following activity students use a relatively small set of sources in order to compare and contrast two singing groups with whom they are likely unfamiliar. Rather than just saying that the groups are similar and different in various ways, the students choose one singing group over another based on their comparison and contrast.

EPISODE 6.1.   Give your students the following task: You and a group of friends are attending a small musical festival with two sound stages. The second set features two groups with which you are not familiar: the Bobs and the Persuasions. (These are real groups.) Each group sings *a cappella*—that is, without musical accompaniment. While similar in many ways, there are key differences between the two. You need to choose which of the two performances you will attend. Fortunately, the music program you bought as a souvenir includes descriptions of both bands.

Figures 1–5 and 1–6 describe the two singing groups. Tell the students they may also use the Internet to get additional information to help them make their decision. As they work, circulate among the groups, monitoring their work and answering their questions.

EPISODE 6.2.   Have the members of each group use the notes they have taken to explain to the others which performance they have decided to see. As students comment on or question their classmates' thinking (different groups will most likely have developed different procedures for using their source material), groups will hold to or revise their decision.

A hallmark of a structured process approach is that students often *develop procedures inductively*. Rather than modeling a way to do things, teachers develop activities that require problem-framing and problem-solving discussions through which students develop procedures and approaches appropriate to the task. Groups of students who have worked together then talk with other groups and share their thinking about the task, thus expanding everyone's ideas.

Figure 1–5. Who Are the Bobs?

The Bobs
Official website: www.bobs.com/

The Bobs are a "new wave" *a cappella* group that originally came from San Francisco. At the time of their formation, the members of the band delivered singing telegrams, but when Western Union folded in 1981, they became unemployed. Gunnar Madsen and Matthew Stull were among these now-out-of-work singers. They loved singing together and wanted to form an *a cappella* singing group so they could continue singing for a living. They placed a small classified advertisement looking for a bass singer and got one call, from Richard "Bob" Greene, who not only sang bass but also wrote songs and had experience as a recording engineer.

Their first show was at an open mike in a Cuban restaurant where they sang "Psycho Killer" by the Talking Heads, "Helter Skelter" by the Beatles, and other songs rarely sung by *a cappella* groups. The audience found them different and amusing and responded enthusiastically. In their other early shows they sang other popular songs with new and innovative arrangements, but soon they began writing their own material, also with unusual arrangements. These new songs often required an additional voice. As they began writing their own songs,

Figure 1–5. Who Are the Bobs? (*continued*)

they realized that they needed to add another singer. They held auditions and discovered Janie "Bob" Scott, who joined the group and helped to polish their performances.

The name Bobs is of uncertain origin. It might be an acronym for Best of Breed, which is an award given out at dog shows for the overall winner of the show. Or it might be a short version of the Oral Bobs. Or it might be something else. In any case, although none of the singers is actually named Bob, all use Bob for a middle name.

Kaleidoscope Records in San Francisco produced their first album, *The Bobs*. They got a Grammy nomination for their version of "Helter Skelter," which also won a Contemporary A Cappella Recording Award (CARA) in 1992. Their award was presented with the following comments: "Rather than translating instrumental parts to voices or relying on clichéd syllables and voicings, Gunnar and Richard created a new vocabulary of sounds and textures. The arrangement deconstructs the song line by line, transforming the Beatles classic into an *a cappella*, postmodern performance art piece." This recognition helped launch a national tour; they also received exposure on radio and television, and embarked on tours across the U.S. and Europe, including performances at major music festivals. They have since won numerous CARA awards.

Since their early success, the Bobs have written songs on many odd and witty topics. These include cattle farming on the moon, doing laundry, Watergate villains, graffiti, security guards at shopping malls, cats who want to conquer the world, tattoos, spontaneous human combustion, heart transplants, bus drivers, violence at the post office, and other amusing curiosities. Furthermore, their *a cappella* arrangements are very unusual. Some have called their performances a cross between the Barenaked Ladies and the Manhattan Transfer.

(*continues*)

Figure 1–5. Who Are the Bobs? (*continued*)

While most of their music is *a cappella*, they have included toy drums, technology that distorts their voices, a piano, clapping, and occasional rock band accompaniment. But since they formed in 1981 they have primarily sung *a cappella* music. While never a widespread commercial success, they have developed a healthy cult following that has kept them performing and recording for over 25 years. Their fans rewarded them by attending several concerts in 2006 to celebrate the 25th Anniversary of the Bobs, in which seven of the eight singers from the band's history performed. A documentary film about their first quarter-century together, *Sign My Snarling Movie: 25 Years of the Bobs*, was released in 2007.

The Bobs have not been content simply with singing. They have also worked with dance companies. They wrote a series of songs, "The Laundry Cycle," for the Oberlin Dance Collective in 1987. At around the same time they met the dance troupe Momix, later known as ISO. Their collaboration was known for its improvisation and creativity. This work attracted the attention of Lincoln Center, which resulted in a show on public television and recognition in the Smithsonian Institute's Museum of American History. They have also provided the majority of the soundtrack for the 1996 film *For Better or Worse*, and during the televised Emmy Award program, they performed a medley of television themes with former *Seinfeld* co-star Jason Alexander.

The band's membership has completely turned over since the original quartet. Co-founder Gunnar "Bob" Madsen retired in 1990, and was replaced by Joe "Bob" Finetti for a thirteen-year run with the band. Other changes in personnel occurred as well. The group has therefore both evolved and remained true to its core principles of performing musically adroit yet wacky lyrics, sound effects, and arrangements for a highly entertaining effect. The *Bergen (NJ) Record/Home News Tribune* called

Figure 1–5. Who Are the Bobs? (*continued*)

the Bobs "One of the most entertaining acts on the live circuit today."

Original members:

- Matthew "Bob" Stull
- Gunnar "Bob" Madsen
- Richard "Bob" Greene
- Janie "Bob" Scott

In-between members:

- Lori "Bob" Rivera
- Joe "Bob" Finetti

Current members:

- Richard "Bob" Greene
- Matthew "Bob" Stull
- Amy "Bob" Engelhardt
- Dan "Bob" Schumacher

Figure 1–6. Who Are the Persuasions?

The Persuasions
Official website: www.thepersuasions.net/

The Persuasions are an *a cappella* singing group that formed in Brooklyn in 1962. The group has had a very stable membership over the years, although the personnel have changed as the band has aged (and in one case, died). Jerry Lawson, who left the group in 2003 to do charitable work and perform solo, was a founding member and sang lead vocals for over four decades. Second

(continues)

Figure 1–6. Who Are the Persuasions? (*continued*)

tenor "Sweet" Joe Russell has sung the high range of the arrangements for most of the group's history, although he took a leave of absence due to illness at one point and presently is the Persuasions' lead singer. Jimmy Hayes has been a stalwart as the group's bass singer and has occasionally sung lead vocals on songs such as "Sixty Minute Man." Jayotis Washington sings tenor and occasional lead and has also been with the group since its founding, with a brief departure from which he returned. Herbert "Tuobo" Rhodes, an original Persuasion who sang harmonies in the baritone range, died in 1988 while the band was touring.

During the core members' absences from the band, others have filled their roles in the group's harmonies. Temporary Persuasions have included Bernard Jones, Willie C. Daniels, and Beverly Rohlehr, the band's only female member, who briefly filled in for Joe Russell and sang high harmonies. Ray Sanders and Reggie Moore (who replaced Jerry Lawson) have joined the band on a permanent basis, rounding out the remaining original members Jayotis Washington, Jimmy Hayes, and Joe Russell. For the most part the Persuasions have included five singers, but have toured and recorded albums with four during various members' leaves of absence from the band and following Tuobo Rhodes' death.

The Persuasions have released about twenty albums over the course of their 45-plus year history and have performed on stages all over the world. They have performed concerts on their own and have also opened for Frank Zappa and the Mothers of Invention, Joni Mitchell, Ray Charles, Bill Cosby, Richard Pryor, and other major stars. And early in their careers, Roseanne Barr and Bruce Springsteen opened for the Persuasions. They have also recorded and performed with a diverse array of musicians, including Stevie Wonder, Bette Midler, Liza Minelli, Van Morrison, Lou Reed, Gladys Knight, Patti LaBelle, Little Richard,

Figure 1–6. Who Are the Persuasions? (*continued*)

Nancy Wilson, the Neville Brothers, Country Joe McDonald, B. B. King, and Paul Simon. Not only have they kept distinguished company, they have performed at levels at least as high as those of their friends and collaborators.

The Persuasions' music is grounded in gospel, soul, doo-wop, and rhythm and blues music, although they have also performed music from other genres. They have written little music of their own, choosing instead to interpret songs from other composers' catalogues. Their songs have come from the African American church, Motown, soul artists such as Sam Cooke (their most important influence), Elvis Presley, and others. Even when the song they sing was originally not soulful, their performance of it always is. More recently they have dedicated whole albums to the music of significant artists, including CDs featuring the music of the Beatles, Frank Zappa, U2, and the Grateful Dead. They have also released albums centering on gospel music and children's songs. In every case their music is inspired, soulful, and filled with energy and humor.

The Persuasions are considered by many to be the epitome of *a cappella* music, especially in the area of doo-wop, soul, and gospel-inspired music. Many groups list them among their most important influences, including Take 6, the Nylons, Rockapella, and Boys II Men. In many ways they are responsible for the survival of *a cappella* music outside the confines of barbershops and college choral groups. The secret to their success is that they have not sold out. They did record one album with musical accompaniment but abandoned the experiment and returned to their roots for the remainder of their history. No matter what the source of their music—Rogers and Hammerstein, Bob Dylan, Clyde McPhatter, or children's songs—they infuse the music with their wit, charm,

(*continues*)

Figure 1–6. Who Are the Persuasions? (*continued*)

energy, and soaring harmonies. They have taken songs from across the musical spectrum and reinvented them as pure Persuasions creations.

In the 1990s Persuasions admirer Fred Parnes produced the documentary film *Spread the Word: The Persuasions Sing A Cappella*, which has been warmly embraced by the Persuasions' many admirers. Their music has appeared in film soundtracks as diverse as *Joe Versus the Volcano, The Heartbreak Kid, Streets of Gold,* and *E.T. the Extraterrestrial*. They have also appeared on several television specials, including Spike Lee's *Do It A Cappella* (in which they were described as "the godfathers of *a cappella*") and the public television special *Music of the Late Kurt Weill*. They have additionally sung on *Good Morning America,* the *Today Show,* the *Tonight Show, Saturday Night Live!,* and *Late Night with Conan O' Brien*.

The Persuasions keep on keepin' on, weathering changes in personnel and the ever fickle public taste in music. They have endured because of their love for their work and their talent in choosing material, arranging it, and singing it with gusto. They are truly the Godfathers of *A Cappella,* the Kings of *A Cappella,* and every other accolade bestowed upon them since the early 1960s. May they sing forever.

Extensions

1. Reemploy some of the processes used in previous stages and episodes of the sequence. For instance, if students have trouble generating content, conduct additional small-group sessions devoted to coming up with ideas. Or have students individually write about ideas they have produced as a group. Or have groups give and receive additional peer feedback before writing final drafts.

2. If a comparison/contrast essay appears on a state- or districtwide writing test, have students write comparison/contrast essays on topics and under conditions that mimic those on the test.

3. Feature comparison/contrast essays in a conceptual unit (see Smagorinsky 2008 and www.coe.uga.edu/~smago /VirtualLibrary/Unit_Outlines.htm) centered on a theme (e.g., gender roles), genre (e.g., allegory), archetype (e.g., the folk hero), reading strategy (e.g., understanding point of view), single author's works (e.g., the works of Alice Walker), movement (e.g., the Black Arts Movement), period (e.g., the British Restoration), or region (e.g., the authors of Arizona). Students can compare and contrast:

    • Authors within a category (e.g., Haki Madhubuti and Nikki Giovanni, Jack Kerouac and Allen Ginsberg).

    • Characters within a work (e.g., Huck Finn and Tom Sawyer, Macbeth and Lady Macbeth).

    • Characters in related texts (e.g., Tartuffe and Volpone, Ozymandius and Miniver Cheevy).

    • Songs related to unit concepts (e.g., in a unit on "the journey," Johnny Clegg and Savuka's "Spirit is the Journey" and Joni Mitchell's "Woodstock"; in a unit on discrimination, Harry Belafonte's "Kwela (Listen to the Man)" and the Dave Matthews Band's "Cry Freedom."

    • Film and literary versions of the same text (e.g., the film and graphic novel versions of *V for Vendetta*; *Romeo and Juliet* and *West Side Story*).

    • Different perspectives on the same concept or event (e.g., Michael Franti and Spearhead's "Light Up Ya Lighter" and Toby Keith's "Courtesy of the Red, White, & Blue (The Angry American)."

    • Two legendary heroes from literature. A student example from Angela's class is provided in Figure 1–7.

Figure 1–7. Fernando's Essay: Heroes

A hero is a person that helps other people. Heroes are strong, brave, loyal, and smart. A real hero doesn't need to have super powers. They just need to help and do good for their people and their city. Lancelot is more of a hero than Arthur.

King Arthur was a strong leader, generous, and in love. For example, he was a strong leader because he fought at the end instead of obeying Malagant and showed pride to his people. He also led his men into fighting Malagant's army. He was generous by letting Lancelot join and become a knight at the round table. This shows that he's willing to trust others and he wants protection from a brave knight. King Arthur is in love with Guinevere because he sends a lot of his men to get her. They will bring her back to Camelot so Arthur can marry her. As you can see, King Arthur could be a good hero because he's strong, generous, but he's not as good as Lancelot.

Lancelot is brave, loyal, and is in love with Guinevere. For example, he's brave because he doesn't fear death and he likes to fight a lot. He also fights 10 men at the same time and he kills them all and he's not afraid of anyone or anything. He's also loyal because he accepted King Arthur's invitation and joined the round table to protect his king. Also, when Malagant attacked, he protected his city by killing about 50 men. Lancelot is in love with Guinevere because he went after Guinevere when she was kidnapped by Malagant and saves her. He also kept pursuing her after she rejected him. In the end, Lancelot is more of a hero because he has all of a hero's characteristics.

Lancelot is more of a hero than Arthur. They both have some hero characteristics. Heroes can have flaws, but they have to fight it and not lose. We know that nobody is perfect, so heroes can have flaws. We need heroes because they make the world a better and safer place to live.

Summing Up

This sequence of activities illustrates many features of a structured process approach. In class, the students do the work as they talk and write about the materials provided.

The activities scaffold students' progression through a series of increasingly complex tasks, beginning with topics volunteered by the students and concluding with unfamiliar topics requiring the students to consult source material. Always, however, the students are able to base their thinking and writing on concrete data; they do not fabricate the content of their writing.

The activities are highly social and include whole-group and small-group discussions at every stage of instruction. These discussions allow the students to try out ideas and engage in exploratory talk through which they may develop new insights. Their initial efforts at composing are done collaboratively; students get immediate feedback on their efforts and receive help shaping their understanding of the topic and expressing their beliefs.

The emphasis throughout is on learning procedures for comparing and contrasting. Although every group doesn't necessarily develop identical procedures, each group is introduced to other groups' processes and can borrow those procedures. The language lesson focuses on procedures as well; students combine sentences to create complex sentences juxtaposing two ideas rather being asked to recognize errors in someone else's writing.

Ultimately, the emphasis on procedures gives students a tool kit for expanding their options when writing comparison/contrast essays. Appropriate extensions help students reapply these procedures, thus reinforcing their understanding of how to use them as they develop as writers.

Teaching Comparison/ Contrast Writing in a Unit on Point of View

Although there are times when writing is taught as an end in itself, students often write while studying other strands in the curriculum. Writing is always best taught in some sort of context: as a genuine expression of personally important ideas addressed to people who care to learn them, as a measure of writing competence on state exams, as a way to think about or be accountable for the reading of literature, and so on. Many effective teachers also embed grammar and syntax in their students' writing instruction (see Weaver 1996, for example).

In much of our other work (for example, Hillocks et al. 1971; Smagorinsky 2008) we advocate embedding writing instruction in the English curriculum as a series of concept explorations tied together with *curricular conversations* (Applebee 1996): rich classroom talk across a variety of contexts that has an overall purpose, thrust, and theme.

The junior year American literature curriculum, for instance, might address the idea of the American dream in eight or ten units (four or five a semester), each covering four to six weeks, formed around topics perhaps selected from the following menu: the Puritan ethic, protest literature, materialism and success, progress and technology, social responsibility, the individual and society, satire, gender roles, justice, frontier literature, changing times, the banality of evil, the family, immigration, the frontier, propaganda, discrimination, cultural conflict, the Harlem Renaissance, Transcendentalism, authors of Mississippi, and the poems of Emily Dickinson. This approach departs from the conventional way of teaching American literature in chronological order. It allows you to cluster works from specific literary periods that share themes and other key motifs. At www.coe.uga.edu/~smago/VirtualLibrary/Unit_Outlines.htm there is a large (and ever-growing) collection of conceptual unit ideas, often accompanied by specific lesson plans. Organizing instruction around a concept helps students trace an idea through a series of texts, each leading to a better understanding of both the previous one and the next one.

A comparison and contrast essay can be part of any conceptual instructional unit, whatever the organizational category. For example:

- *Themes.* In a unit on *the family*, students could compare and contrast fictional families, focusing on economic context (e.g., comparing the circumstances of the various families in Dickens' *David Copperfield* and how they affect their members' life prospects), gender roles (e.g., comparing family member roles in the Dick and Jane series and in the Berenstain Bears series, or in more complex stories such as Alice Walker's *The Color Purple*), the role of religious faith (e.g., comparing the different interpretations of Zionism by the Saunders and Malter families in Chaim Potok's *The Chosen*), and other features of family life.

- *Genres or archetypes.* In a unit on science fiction, students could compare and contrast two different visions of the future (e.g., one in which humans grow weaker, as in H. G. Wells' *The Time Machine*, and one in which humanity grows more enlightened, as in Robert Heinlein's *Stranger in a Strange Land*), two perspectives on technology (e.g., Isaac Asimov's optimistic conception in *I, Robot* and Margaret Atwood's dystopian view in *Oryx and Crake*), or two views of the human relationship with nature (e.g., Ursula Le Guin's

environmentally friendly *The Word for World Is Forest* and
Cormack McCarthy's apocalyptic *The Road*).

- *Reading strategies.* For a unit on *propaganda*, students could
  compare and contrast two propaganda efforts on the same
  issue from different perspectives (e.g., comparing and contrasting different political advertisements for opposing
  candidates for the same office) or different uses of the same
  propaganda strategy (e.g., different uses of the *black-and-white
  fallacy*—"you're either with us or against us"—in politics).

- *Literary periods.* Students could compare and contrast two
  authors from the same period, such as two poets from the
  Harlem Renaissance (e.g., Countee Cullen and Langston
  Hughes), two orators or authors from the U.S. Colonial/
  Revolutionary period (e.g., Patrick Henry and Thomas Paine),
  or two poets from the British Victorian period (e.g., Emily
  Bronte and Christina Rossetti).

- *Movements.* Students could compare and contrast two move-
  ments of the same type (e.g., U.S. Romanticism and British
  Romanticism), two related movements (e.g., Realism and
  Naturalism), two authors from related movements (e.g.,
  Maya Angelou from the Black Arts Movement and Zora Neale
  Hurston from the Harlem Renaissance), or two authors from
  the same movement (e.g., the confessional poets Sylvia Plath
  and Anne Sexton).

- *Regions.* Students could compare and contrast writers from
  the same region (e.g., British lake poets Samuel Taylor
  Coleridge and William Wordsworth), general trends between
  the writers of different regions (e.g., differences between
  Great Lakes fiction and Southern fiction), or specific authors
  who demonstrate differences between two regional styles
  (e.g., the slave narratives of Cuba's Juan Manzano and the
  U.S. South's Harriet Jacobs).

- *Particular authors.* Students could compare and contrast different works by the same author (e.g., two short stories by

Edgar Allan Poe), works from different periods of an author's life (e.g., George Orwell's 1933 *Down and Out in Paris and London* and his 1949 *Nineteen Eighty-Four*), or attitudes toward different subjects (e.g., Shakespeare's portrayal of women in *The Taming of the Shrew* and Jews in *The Merchant of Venice*).

- *Points of view.* Students could compare and contrast the perspectives of two characters whose actions are related by a single narrator (e.g., Nick Carraway's portrayal of Jay Gatsby and Tom Buchanan in *Fitzgerald's The Great Gatsby*), those of two narrators within the same work (e.g., Darl and Cash in Faulkner's *As I Lay Dying*), those of two commentators on the same issue or events (e.g., the narrator of *Beowulf* and the narrator of John Gardner's *Grendel*), or those of a work's author and the work's narrator (e.g., Mark Twain and Huck Finn in Twain's *The Adventures of Huckleberry Finn*).

The lesson sequence in this chapter teaches the comparison/contrast essay in the context of a unit on point of view. The unit is designed for ninth graders but could be adapted to other grade levels.

Task and Activity Analysis

The following outline demonstrates how literary anthologies and textbooks often itemize elements related to *narrative point of view*:

1. Narrative points of view

    - First person

    - First person omniscient

    - Second person

    - Third person

    - Multiple person

    - Alternating person

2. Narrative voice

   - Stream-of-consciousness

   - Character

     - Reliable

     - Unreliable

   - Epistolary

   - Third person

     - Subjective

     - Objective

     - Omniscient

3. Narrative tense

   - Past

   - Present

   - Future

4. Narrative modes

   - Fiction

   - Other

Textbooks usually approach point of view in terms of the type of narration the author has chosen. However, classifying Huck Finn as an unreliable first-person past-tense narrator doesn't help an adolescent reader grasp the meaning of Huck's perspective. Understanding his point of view relies on the ability to recognize Huck's narration as a creation of author Mark Twain. Twain, we presume, is asking the reader to judge Huck's views on different aspects of his adventures: his family, his companion Jim, civilization and those who inhabit it, the river, and so on. We believe *applying procedural knowledge related to content* (knowing *how* to understand the meaning of the text) is a better approach. The following lesson sequence, while taking into account the formal aspects of literary perspective, relies on knowing *how to use that knowledge* to achieve a meaningful reading.

The comparison/contrast process laid out in Chapter 1 applies here as well:

- Identify the instances of comparison and contrast between the two points of view.

- Characterize each point of view in terms of instances of comparison and contrast.

- Create priorities among the instances of comparison and contrast.

- Compare and contrast the two points of view.

- Make a value judgment.

The activities in this unit help students learn how to (1) understand how and why people see things differently and (2) communicate this understanding in a comparison/contrast essay.

Stage 1. Assess Students' Knowledge of Comparing and Contrasting

If you are teaching the comparison/contrast essay for the first time, you may want to assess what your students already know about this kind of thinking and writing.

EPISODE 1.1. Give students the following assignment: Think of one person, place, thing, or event that is viewed differently by two people or two types of people. For instance:

- Conservatives and liberals might view the same politician differently.

- Fans of two competing teams might view the same athlete differently.

- People with different musical tastes might view the same musician differently.

- People with different senses of taste might view the same restaurant differently.

- People with different priorities might view the same item (car, house, clothing, etc.) differently.

Compare and contrast the points of view of two people or two groups of people on the topic you chose above, making sure to:

- Identify the instances of comparison and contrast.

- Characterize each point of view in terms of the instances of comparison and contrast.

- Create priorities among the instances of comparison and contrast.

- Compare and contrast the two points of view.

- Make a value judgment.

EPISODE 1.2. Evaluate these initial comparison/contrast essays using the rubric in Figure 2–1 and plan your instruction accordingly. The lesson sequence here focuses on each aspect of learning how to write a comparison/contrast essay on different narrative perspectives in literary texts.

Stage 2. Gateway Activity: Call Attention to Different Narrative Perspectives

EPISODE 2.1. Identify an incident involving a conflict between peer groups in your school or in a school in the news. For simple mayhem, the website www.schoolfightsdump.com/ includes videos of physical fights taking place in schools, mostly between students but involving teachers and parents as well. Students clash over shared romantic interests, turf, social differences, neighborhood affiliations, racial differences, socioeconomic differences, and much else. Finding a conflict in either your school or another shouldn't require a great deal of searching.

Figure 2–1. Rubric for Assessing Students' Initial Comparison/Contrast Essays

	5 CLEARLY ACCOMPLISHED	4 ACCOMPLISHED YET LACKING PRECISION OR CLARITY OF EXPRESSION	3 ATTEMPTED AND ACCOMPLISHED BUT LACKING DETAIL	2 ATTEMPTED BUT WITH UNCLEAR RESULTS	1 NOT ATTEMPTED
An introductory paragraph clearly states the purpose of the essay and the major points covered.					
The body paragraphs compare and contrast instances that clearly distinguish the two observers' perspectives.					
A concluding paragraph or paragraphs make a value judgment about the two observers based on the comparison and contrast.					

Once the class agrees on an incident to study, divide the students into groups, each group taking on the role of one of participants in the conflict. For example:

- a student from one of the social groups involved in the incident
- a student from the opposing social group
- members of the school security or disciplinary force
- the school principal
- a teacher (real or hypothetical) present during the incident
- a member of a social group not directly involved in the incident.

EPISODE 2.2. Have each group recount the incident from the perspective of their character. Leave the medium up to them. They could write a story narrated by their character, write and possibly perform a play depicting the events through the eyes of their character, create a computer animation of the events, convey the events through a puppet show, or develop some other presentation.

EPISODE 2.3. Have each group present its recounting to the class, so everyone sees the event played out from several points of view. Following the presentations, consider these questions:

- Is there an objective way to view the incident?

- How is each participant's actions and perspective justified?

- How is each participant's actions a function of a social group identity?

- How do the participants position themselves relative to other participants?

- In what ways do the participants both understand and misunderstand one another?

- What efforts have the participants made to empathize with one another?

- What might be gained and lost from extending such empathy?

- To what extent is there compathy—the act of feeling with someone else—among the participants, and what are the consequences of this degree of compathy?

EPISODE 2.4. Have students, in small groups, compare and contrast two of the perspectives presented. Give the following instructions:

Choose any two of the perspectives developed by the class for the opening activity. Compare and contrast these perspectives. Outline the elements of your comparison (things that are similar) and contrast (things that are different). Use the following graphic organizers to capture your findings. (Complete them in number order.)

Organizer 1: Similarities Between Perspectives (Comparison)

Identify areas in which the participants have similar perspectives: physical view of the events, prejudices, agendas, ability to perceive things clearly, personal background, emotional makeup, psychological makeup, moral constitution, etc.

	PERSPECTIVE OF PARTICIPANT A	PERSPECTIVE OF PARTICIPANT B
Similarity 1		
Similarity 2		
Similarity 3		
Similarity 4		
Similarity 5		
Similarity 6		
Similarity 7		

Organizer 2: Differences Between Perspectives (Contrast)

Identify areas in which the participants have different perspectives: physical view of the events, prejudices, agendas, ability to perceive things clearly, personal background, emotional makeup, psychological makeup, moral constitution, etc.

	PERSPECTIVE OF PARTICIPANT A	PERSPECTIVE OF PARTICIPANT B
Difference 1		
Difference 2		
Difference 3		
Difference 4		
Difference 5		
Difference 6		
Difference 7		

Organizer 3: Choosing Features to Compare and Contrast

1. Discuss which similarities and differences best help you understand and explain the perspectives in relation to one another. A
   feature that helps form the participants' perspectives (e.g., one
   is sympathetic to one type of person, the other is sympathetic to
   another type of person) is more useful than a feature that does
   not (e.g., the relative bushiness of their eyebrows).

2. In the first column, list the instances of comparison and contrast
   that are most important in understanding and explaining the
   participants' perspectives; in the second and third columns, list
   aspects of each similarity/difference that affect each participant's
   perspective. (There is space for five instances of comparison/con-
   trast. Your analysis may produce more, or fewer; add rows as
   necessary.)

Area of Comparison/ Contrast	Aspects That Affect Participant A's Perspective	Aspects That Affect Participant B's Perspective
1.		
2.		
3.		
4.		
5.		

Organizer 4: Value Judgment and Reasons

1. State a value judgment about the two participants' perspectives (e.g.,
   participant A had a clearer view and does not have a personal interest in the outcome of the incident, and so participant A's perspective
   should be believed over participant B's).

2. Explain in detail why you have reached this conclusion.

Value Judgment:

REASONS:

1.

2.

3.

4.

5.

EPISODE 2.5. Have each group present their analysis to the class (using presentation software or other technology if doing so is feasible). After each presentation, let students from other groups ask questions, raise concerns, take issue with conclusions, and otherwise critique and discuss the findings. This discussion helps students clarify the work they have done and sharpen their understanding of the different perspectives they have analyzed.

EPISODE 2.6. (OPTIONAL) If time permits, have each small group collaboratively compose an essay based on their planning and the feedback they have received from their classmates. By writing a group composition on a relatively accessible problem, students gain experience before taking on more complex literary comparisons and contrasts. The more practice at each stage of the learning process, the more fluent performances at later, more challenging stages will be. (When the groups have completed their essays, each group could exchange essays with another group, apply the grading rubric, revise the essay, and turn it in to you for evaluation.)

Give the following assignment:

Use the information from your planning and discussions to write a group composition comparing and contrasting two participants' perspectives on the same event:

1. In the first paragraph (the introduction), state what you are comparing and explain the major issues you will discuss.
2. In the next set of paragraphs (the body of your essay), explain how each participant is positioned according to each major category of comparison and contrast. Provide as many details as are necessary to argue persuasively for the value judgment you ultimately reach. Provide a separate paragraph (or set of paragraphs) for each instance of comparison and contrast you address.
3. In the final paragraph(s), state your value judgment and explain how you arrived at it based on your analysis in the body of your essay.

Choose your potential audience from among the following sets of readers:

1. members of each social group involved to help them understand the situation
2. members of the school's conflict resolution team to give them a better understanding of the conflict and its origins
3. the school principal, who must make a disciplinary decision about the incident
4. readers of the school newspaper as part of a story about the incident
5. members of the board of education as a way to inform their development of a new policy regarding student conflicts.

Your essay will be assessed using this rubric:

	5 CLEARLY ACCOMPLISHED	4 ACCOMPLISHED YET LACKING PRECISION OR CLARITY OF EXPRESSION	3 ATTEMPTED AND ACCOMPLISHED BUT LACKING DETAIL	2 ATTEMPTED BUT WITH UNCLEAR RESULTS	1 NOT ATTEMPTED
An introductory paragraph clearly states the purpose of the essay and the major points you will cover.					
Body paragraphs compare and contrast instances that clearly distinguish the two characters' perspectives.					
A concluding paragraph or paragraphs make a value judgment about the two participants based on the comparison and contrast.					

Stage 3. Present a Language Lesson on Conjunctive Adverbs

A language lesson can be included at many points in the sequence. The lesson in Figure 2–2 on using and punctuating conjunctive adverbs to introduce both comparisons and contrasts helps students make their points clearly to their readers. Depending on your circumstances, this lesson could be taught later in the sequence instead.

Figure 2–2. Using Conjunctive Adverbs for Comparison/Contrast

Conjunctive adverbs are words that help you combine statements into a fluid sentence that helps you make your points clearly. Typically, a conjunctive adverb appears between and connects two independent clauses. Usually a semicolon appears before the conjunctive adverb, and a comma follows it. The following sentences illustrate their usage:

For comparison: Amelia Chowdown wasn't wearing her glasses and couldn't see clearly; *similarly*, Dylan Parsley had an object in his eye and his vision was obscured.

For contrast: Baron Landscape was prejudiced because he didn't like people with red hair; *in contrast*, Felton Earthquake loved everyone and so saw the situation without bias.

There are other kinds of conjunctive adverbs, but for this exercise we will focus on the following:

For making comparisons: *also, in the same way, likewise, similarly*

For making contrasts: *although, and yet, at the same time, but at the same time, despite that, even so, even though, for all that, however, in contrast, in spite of, instead, nevertheless, notwithstanding, on the contrary, on the other hand, otherwise, regardless, still, though, yet*

Each item below contains two sentences. Combine them into one sentence by inserting a conjunctive adverb between them, preceded by a semicolon (;) and followed by a comma (,). Decide whether you are making a comparison or a contrast, and use a word from the appropriate set to combine the two sentences into one.

1. Izzy Serious believes that space aliens landed at Roswell, New Mexico, in 1947. Kareem O'Wheat thinks that the alleged incident is a hoax.

Figure 2–2. Using Conjunctive Adverbs for Comparison/Contrast
(*continued*)

2. Izzy doesn't trust the government. Kareem believes that the government would never hide important information from its citizens.

3. Izzy has never taken a science course. Kareem won his school's "Science Stud of the Year" award.

4. Izzy is a regular reader of news found at supermarket checkout counters. Kareem began subscribing to *Scientific American* when he was 3 years old.

5. Izzy has watched every episode of *The X-Files*. Kareem has watched every episode twice.

6. Izzy finds evidence of debris from the crash to be persuasive. Kareem believes that the debris came from a weather balloon.

7. Izzy believes that autopsies of dead aliens were conducted following the crash of the space ship. Kareem thinks that the mortician who claims to have conducted them is lying or deranged.

8. Izzy believes the witnesses who claim to have seen the crash. Kareem insists that these witnesses saw other atmospheric phenomena.

9. Izzy believes that the government has covered up many other conspiracies, such as the Kennedy assassination. Kareem trusts the government always to be honest and forthcoming.

10. Izzy is concerned about disagreements over the exact site of the crash. Kareem finds these disagreements to be troubling.

Stage 4. Analyze Point of View in Simple Stories

Students undertake a relatively simple comparison/contrast of narrative perspectives in different versions of "Red Riding Hood," a tale that has been told from different cultural perspectives and also from the points of view of different characters. The following websites include many different versions of this story, including perspectives of characters other than Red Riding Hood's, such as the grandmother's:

www.pitt.edu/~dash/type0333.html#contents

www.usm.edu/english/fairytales/lrrh/lrrhhome.htm

www.readwritethink.org/lessons/lesson_view.asp?id=889

Versions told from the point of view of the wolf include *The Wolf's Story: What Really Happened to Little Red Riding Hood*, by Toby Forward (Walker Children's, 2006).

EPISODE 4.1. Identify the versions of "Little Red Riding Hood" you will use. For illustrative purposes, we'll use *Little Red Cap*, by Jacob and Wilhelm Grimm (available at www.pitt.edu/~dash/type0333 .html#grimm), and *Little Red Riding Hood Retold*, by Curtis Johnston (available at http://students.ou.edu/J/Curtis.N.Johnston-1/ LittleRedRidingHoodRetold.html). The first is a "classic" version, with Red Cap described as a "sweet little girl" and the wolf as "wicked." In Johnson's version, the wolf narrates the story and describes himself as "gentle" and "kind." Distribute and the stories and have students read them.

EPISODE 4.2. Have students, in small groups, compare and contrast the two perspectives in the narratives. Give these instructions:

Compare and contrast the perspectives of the narrators of the Grimm Brothers and Johnson versions of "Little Red Riding Hood." Outline the elements of your comparison (things that are similar) and contrast (things that are different). Use the following graphic organizers to capture your findings (complete them in number order).

Organizer 1: Similarities Between Perspectives (Comparison)

Identify areas in which the narrators have similar perspectives: physical view of the events, prejudices, agendas, ability to perceive things clearly, personal background, emotional makeup, psychological makeup, moral constitution, etc.

	PERSPECTIVE OF GRIMM NARRATOR	PERSPECTIVE OF JOHNSON NARRATOR
Similarity 1		
Similarity 2		
Similarity 3		
Similarity 4		
Similarity 5		
Similarity 6		
Similarity 7		

Organizer 2: Differences Between Perspectives (Contrast)

Identify areas in which the narrators have different perspectives: physical view of the events, prejudices, agendas, ability to perceive things clearly, personal background, emotional makeup, psychological makeup, moral constitution, etc.

	PERSPECTIVE OF GRIMM NARRATOR	PERSPECTIVE OF JOHNSON NARRATOR
Difference 1		
Difference 2		
Difference 3		
Difference 4		
Difference 5		
Difference 6		
Difference 7		

Organizer 3: Choosing Features to Compare and Contrast

1. Discuss which similarities and differences best help you compare and contrast the two narrators and their perspectives. A feature that helps form a narrator's perspective—one is gynophagic (i.e., devours women), the other does not eat people of any kind—is probably more useful than one that does not—one has a tail, the other does not.

2. In the first column, list the instances of comparison and contrast that are most important in understanding and explaining the narrators' perspectives; in the second and third columns, list aspects of each similarity and difference that affect each narrator's perspective. (There is space for five instances of comparison and contrast. Your analysis may produce more or fewer; add rows as necessary.)

AREA OF COMPARISON/ CONTRAST	ASPECTS THAT AFFECT GRIMM NARRATOR'S PERSPECTIVE	ASPECTS THAT AFFECT JOHNSON NARRATOR'S PERSPECTIVE
1.		
2.		
3.		
4.		
5.		

Organizer 4: Value Judgment and Reasons

1. State a value judgment about the two narrators' perspectives (e.g., the Grimm narrator appears to be a human being, and thus is more sympathetic to Red Riding Hood than is the wolf, who narrates the Johnson version).

2. Explain in detail why you have reached this conclusion.

VALUE JUDGMENT:

REASONS:

1.

2.

3.

4.

5.

EPISODE 4.3. Have each group report their analysis to the class, perhaps using presentation software or other visual aids so that other students can follow their thinking. Ask the class for feedback that will help the group understand which parts of their analysis have been persuasive and which need additional detail and precision.

EPISODE 4.4. Have students write a comparison/contrast essay, either in small groups, with a partner, or independently. Provide the following assignment:

> Use the information from your planning and discussions to write an essay comparing and contrasting the two narrators' perspectives:
>
> 1. In the first paragraph (the introduction), state what you are comparing and explain the major issues you will discuss.
> 2. In the next set of paragraphs (the body of your essay), explain each narrator's position in relation to each major category of comparison and contrast. Provide as many

details as are necessary to argue persuasively for the value judgment you ultimately reach. Provide a separate paragraph (or set of paragraphs) for each instance of comparison and contrast.

3. In the final paragraph or paragraphs, state your value judgment and what in your analysis supports it.

4. Include sentences that use conjunctive adverbs to highlight the comparisons and contrasts.

Your essay will be assessed according to the rubric below.

	5 CLEARLY ACCOMPLISHED	4 ACCOMPLISHED YET LACKING PRECISION OR CLARITY OF EXPRESSION	3 ATTEMPTED AND ACCOMPLISHED BUT LACKING DETAIL	2 ATTEMPTED BUT WITH UNCLEAR RESULTS	1 NOT ATTEMPTED
An introductory paragraph clearly states the purpose of the essay and the major points you will cover.					
Body paragraphs compare and contrast instances that clearly distinguish the two narrators' perspectives.					
A concluding paragraph or paragraphs make a value judgment about the two narrators based on the comparison and contrast.					
You use conjunctive adverbs to highlight comparisons and contrasts within sentences.					

EPISODE 4.5.   Have each group, pair, or individual exchange essays with another group, pair, or individual; apply the grading rubric; revise their essay; and turn it in to you for evaluation.

Stage 5: Conduct an Intermediate Analysis

Students should now be ready for more sophisticated comparisons and contrasts. (If they are not, have them practice these strategies again using relatively familiar material before moving ahead.) The following are possible resources for studying narrative perspective:

1. *Political cartoons.* Liberal and conservative political cartoons commenting on the same current event. Many political cartoons are available at www.gocomics.com/explore /editorials and other online resources. Conservative cartoonists include Bob Gorrell, Dick Locher, Gary Varvel, and many others listed at townhall.com/cartoons/. Liberal cartoonists include Lalo Alcaraz, Tom Toles, and Mike Luckovich.

2. *Political commentary.* Conservative and liberal perspectives on current events. Possible columnists can be found online at the following websites:

    Conservative: www.blogtalkradio.com/politics_ conservative, http://rightwingnews.com/, http:// realclearpolitics.com/

    Liberal: www.Huffingtonpost.com, www.blogtalkradio .com/politics_progressive, www.salon.com, www.talking pointsmemo.com/

3. *Product reviews.* Many online vendors provide reviews that include conflicting opinions of the products they sell. Good sources of product reviews include www .consumersearch.com/, www.amazon.com, www.bizrate .com/, www.comparethebrands.com/, and www.price grabber.com/. One advantage here is that students can investigate different perspectives on products they know

about and might buy, whereas their political perspectives might not be developed enough to make reading political cartoons and columns interesting.

4. *Sports blogs.* Many students follow sports, and fans have different perspectives on every sport, team, and athlete. Sports blogs are available at http://sportsblogs.org/, http://ballhype.com/blogs/, http://sports.yahoo.com /blogs, and http://sports.espn.go.com/espn/blog/main.

5. *Blogs on other topics.* Internet search engines can turn up contrary perspectives on just about anything. If students have particular interests that are not included in the resources above, source material is only a keyword away.

6. *Cultural symbols.* The snake has been interpreted quite differently by different cultures. In the Garden of Eden, the serpent tempts Eve to eat the apple and bring an end to human innocence. In many Native American cultures, snakes symbolize fertility. Snakes have been interpreted by different cultures as signifying deceit, guardianship, rebirth and regeneration, and revenge. Students could analyze different cultural interpretations of the snake or other animal, particularly through cultural narratives, and draw conclusions about how different narrators and the cultures they represent perceive and explain them.

Depending on students' progress, they can again rely on graphic organizers like those used in the gateway and "Little Red Riding Hood" activities.

Stage 6. Analyze Point of View in Harper Lee's *To Kill a Mockingbird*

This sequence was designed by Angela Dean for her high school students. She asked her students to compare and contrast points of view in Harper Lee's *To Kill a Mockingbird*. While limited to the narrative perspective of Jean Louise "Scout" Finch, *To Kill a Mockingbird* provides readers with the points of view of other characters who come into contact with Scout. The book, set in a small Alabama town in the 1930s, examines the Finch family and their neighbors during the time the narrator's father, lawyer Atticus Finch, is facing one of the most difficult cases of his career. Scout, Atticus' daughter, comes of age over the course of the trial and begins to see the many sides of Maycomb and its inhabitants. Given the advice to try and see things from other people's points of view, Scout spends most of the novel confused about how to best understand those around her and how to look beyond her own blind spots while doing so. Many characters interject their views and opinions, giving Scout much to weigh. Through her friends' and neighbors' conversations, declarations, actions, and editorials, Scout finally pieces together what it means to be "fine folks." The many perspectives on the trial, and the society it speaks of, are fertile ground for writing comparison/contrast essays.

EPISODE 6.1. Angela began the lesson sequence after the students had read the first twelve chapters of *To Kill a Mockingbird*. She started by asking students to come up with events that could be considered from multiple points of view. As they called out their ideas, Angela wrote them on the board. Here are some of the ideas they generated:

1. Scout's point of view vs. Jem's point of view when several of Maycomb's male citizens come to see Atticus about moving Tom Robinson to the city jail

2. Scout's point of view vs. Jem's point of view on Atticus' shooting Tim Johnson

3. Aunt Alexandra's point of view vs. Atticus' point of view on raising Scout

4. Scout and Jem's point of view vs. Dill's point of view on Boo Radley

5. Scout and Jem's point of view vs. Calpurnia's point of view on language

6. Atticus' point of view vs. the town's point of view on the trial and Atticus' defense of Tom Robinson.

EPISODE 6.2.   Angela had her students, in pairs, use the graphic organizers below to select a pair of points of view for comparison and contrast.

Organizer 1: Similarities Between Perspectives (Comparison)

Identify areas in which the characters have similar perspectives: physical view of the events, prejudices, agendas, ability to perceive things clearly, personal background, emotional makeup, psychological makeup, moral constitution, etc.

	PERSPECTIVE OF CHARACTER 1	PERSPECTIVE OF CHARACTER 2
Similarity 1		
Similarity 2		
Similarity 3		
Similarity 4		
Similarity 5		
Similarity 6		
Similarity 7		

Organizer 2: Differences Between Perspectives (Contrast)

Identify areas in which the characters have different perspectives: physical view of the events, prejudices, agendas, ability to perceive things clearly, personal background, emotional makeup, psychological makeup, moral constitution, etc.

	PERSPECTIVE OF CHARACTER 1	PERSPECTIVE OF CHARACTER 2
Difference 1		
Difference 2		
Difference 3		
Difference 4		
Difference 5		
Difference 6		
Difference 7		

Organizer 3: Choosing Features to Compare and Contrast

1. Discuss which similarities and differences best help you compare and contrast the two characters and their perspectives. A feature that helps form the characters' perspectives (one is kind to others, the other treats others cruelly; both have the same occupation yet live very different lives) is probably more useful than one that does not (both have nicknames).

2. In the first column, list the instances of comparison and contrast that are most important in understanding and explaining the narrators' perspectives; in the second and third columns, list aspects of each similarity and difference that affect each character's perspective. (There is space for five instances of comparison and contrast. Your analysis may produce more or fewer; add rows as necessary.)

AREA OF COMPARISON/ CONTRAST	ASPECTS THAT AFFECT CHARACTER 1'S PERSPECTIVE	ASPECTS THAT AFFECT CHARACTER 2'S PERSPECTIVE
1.		
2.		
3.		
4.		
5.		

Organizer 4: Value Judgment and Reasons

1. State a value judgment about the two narrators' perspectives (e.g., the narrator who was an alcoholic was a better person than the narrator who occupied a respectable position in town).

1. Explain in detail why you have reached this conclusion.

VALUE JUDGMENT:

REASONS:

1.

2.

3.

4.

5.

EPISODE 6.3. At the end of this initial comparison and contrast, Angela collected and evaluated the groups' work. She noticed that students were evaluating characters but were not supporting their claims with specific examples from the text. Instead, they were making sweeping claims, such as "Aunt Alexandra is judgmental" and "Atticus is understanding." Angela wanted the students to provide the details that show how these statements might be true by using evidence from the text. She also wanted to be sure the students had a good working definition for value judgment and how to formulate one. Therefore, she presented a minilesson based on her observations.

Then, putting students back into their original groups, she had them co-construct their value judgments and begin to support them with evidence from the text, revising where they may have been vague in their first collaboration. Pressed for time because of the approach of end-of-course district tests, Angela allowed students to work together initially, then asked them to finish on their own as homework.

EPISODE 6.4. Next, Angela and her students continued their study of the novel by reading about the trial. Angela asked her students, for homework, to write a series of perspective pieces in their journals each night. She included this task in part as a review of the day's reading and also to accustom the students to considering points of view. They had to take into consideration what they knew about the character they had selected prior to his or her appearance in the courthouse. This information might be extensive (what they knew about the Ewells and the social hierarchy of Maycomb) or limited (what they knew about Tom Robinson and the crime of which he has been accused).

At the beginning of each class period, students shared their pieces with partners, who would try to guess which character's point of view was being presented. Finally, students volunteered to read their perspective pieces aloud to the class, and Angela used their details and opinions to stimulate class discussion. The students' writing also provided a basis for making predictions or connections among all the perspective pieces. Figure 2–3 includes samples of the students' writing.

Figure 2–3. Examples of Students' Point-of-View Journal Entries

Student 1

(Jem's POV)
This trial is so interesting! Atticus is doing a great job. Mr. Ewell did it and I'm sure of it! Mr. Ewell thinks he so high and mighty, but Atticus is proving him guilty every minute.

(Scout's POV)
What did Atticus say that left Mayella so upset? And why is Atticus so upset?? This is all so confusing. She seems to try more than the rest of the Ewells do and she seems like she could be a nice person, but something about her makes me feel like she's hiding something.

(continues)

Figure 2–3. Examples of Students' Point-of-View Journal Entries (*continued*)

(Scout's POV)

I'm so confused. It seems so obvious before that Mr. Ewell did it. Now, I'm not so sure. Tom Robison is mighty nervous. He's sweating like he's got something to hide. Maybe he did it. Yeah. Makes sense. He's real nervous. He's testifying against a white woman and his story is making her look like a liar.

Student 2

(Bob Ewell's POV)

"Mr. Robert E. Lee Ewell!" When the judge called me to the stand in court, I was kind of nervous, so I tried to make a joke out of it, but got in trouble and was asked not to do it again. I believe what I saw was the truth, so I told everyone what I saw and remembered. Atticus kept asking me the same questions about Mayella, then out of nowhere, he asked me if I can read and write?? I no idea why me bein' able to read and write makes a difference, so I showed him and the rest of 'em that I could write my name. I took the pen in my left hand and wrote it, then I saw they was all lookin' at me. Tricky lawyers. That Atticus Finch is just like all the rest of 'em.

I better be careful.

(Mayella's POV)

He made me mad. I thought he was mocking me, using words like "Miss" and "ma'am." I don't like Atticus. How could he defend Tom?? They all act like they's high and mighty. He asked me questions about what happened, and I had no problem with telling him that. When he asked me if I loved my father and if I had friends, that's when things got all messed up. My daddy staring at me and all those people waiting to hear what I had to say. They see what they want to see. Then he started speeding up his questions,

Figure 2–3. Examples of Students' Point-of-View Journal Entries (*continued*)

making me having to reply real quick and not think about my answers, well, I just stopped answerin' him. That made me real mad.

(Tom's POV)
Mr. Finch asked me what happened. I sho' was nervous. I was happy to have my chance, but to say all of that in font of all them children and ladies. It was hard. She looked like she jus needed someone to help her out on that place, like she was real lonely. I don't know why she would say I was the one that jumped on her, when it was the other way around. What if they don't believe me? What if they don't even listen? Why would they listen to me, a Black man? Hump. I gotta find a way out of this. I sho' hope Mr. Finch can convince them that I didn't do it. I know I ran and I know that makes me look guilty, but at that moment I wan't afraid of being blamed. I was running fo my life.

EPISODE 6.5. Once the class had finished reading and discussing the trial, Angela had students examine the trial using the same graphic organizers they used to look at events in Chapters 1–12. Working at tables of four, students either:

- compared and contrasted Atticus' treatment of Mayella on the stand with Mr. Gilmer's treatment of Tom on the stand, or

- looked more closely at similarities and differences between how Mayella and Tom behaved on the stand, what they said on the stand, and what students knew about them as characters.

After choosing one of these two options, students collaborated on ideas and completed the comparisons and contrasts. Figures 2–4 and 2–5 are examples of one group's work.

Figure 2–4. Example of Atticus/Mr Gilmer Comparisons

	ATTICUS	MR. GILMER
Similarity 1	Well educated	Well educated
Similarity 2	Comes from upper/educated class	Comes from upper/educated class
Similarity 3	From Maycomb county	From Maycomb County
Similarity 4	Male	Male
Similarity 5	White	White
Similarity 6	Addresses witnesses in way other than just their first name	Addresses witnesses in way other than just their first name
Similarity 7	With key witness in the cross-examination, asks important questions quickly/climax of cross-examination	With key witness in the cross-examination, asks important questions quickly/climax of cross-examination

Figure 2–5. Example of Atticus/Mr. Gilmer Contrasts

	ATTICUS	MR. GILMER
Difference 1	Polite; calls people with titles of respect—Mr. and Miss	Not very polite; uses the term "boy" to refer to Tom and the "n" word
Difference 2	Patient and becomes impatient (speeds up questions at the end of the cross-examination)	Impatient throughout with Tom's responses, which reinforces beliefs the jury or citizens in the court-room may already have about Tom's guilt/how Black "criminals" should be treated
Difference 3	Defense lawyer	Prosecuting lawyer
Difference 4	Questions show that he's trying to get at the truth	Questions show that he's making accusations toward Tom
Difference 5	Wants the truth from Mayella and has to ask questions that may portray Mayella in a bad way, but doesn't like to do it	Wants to portray Tom in a bad way and seems to not feel shame about how he goes about doing it
Difference 6	Calm, respectful	Hot-headed, hasty, and mocking
Difference 7	Lives in Maycomb	Lives in Abbotsville

EPISODE 6.6.   Using the comparisons and contrasts identified on the first two graphic organizers, the student groups then used graphic organizer 3 to identify what they considered to be the most important issues that distinguished the two perspectives. The student group that prepared the comparison/contrast organizers in Figures 2–4 and 2–5 produced the analysis shown in Figure 2–6.

EPISODE 6.7.   The final step was to consider the gathered information from a particular point of view. Students were allowed to

Figure 2–6. Example Analysis of Atticus'/Mr. Gilmer's Similarities and Differences

AREA OF COMPARISON/ CONTRAST	ATTICUS	MR. GILMER
1. status	White male; highly educated; lives in town; respected and well known by those in the courtroom; defense lawyer	White male; highly educated; lives in Abbotsville; may not be as well known to those in the courtroom who don't usually come to see trials; prosecuting attorney
2. behavior/ treatment of witnesses	Polite and respectful; calm; doesn't really change behavior or treatment of the witness until the very end of his cross-examination when he is trying to catch Mayella in a lie and asks the questions quickly so that he can show she's not telling the truth	Degrading, rushed, and seems hot-headed; treats Tom Robinson with disrespect as soon as he takes the stand; questions are more like accusations throughout the entire cross-examination; uses racist terms to refer to Tom and that work against Tom's image
3. role in case	Defending Tom and works hard at getting at the truth, but finds no joy in treating Mayella like he does at the end of the cross-examination	Prosecuting Tom and doesn't seem to be bothered by his treatment of Tom on the stand
4. view on case	Big case for Atticus; a lot at stake for Tom and for the town; this is the case of his lifetime and one that could have lasting effects on him, his family, and the town	Just another case and just another guilty black man; all about low-class citizens; doesn't matter much to him because he seems confident that the jury will find Tom guilty like they always do

decide if they wanted to write their piece as a diary entry, a letter to a relative living outside Maycomb, or a letter sent to the editor of the *Maycomb Tribune*. Regardless of which form their writing took, they needed to consider the way their characters would act on the stand, including which evidence they believed important, and to include a value judgment.

Working in their groups, students made their selections and collaborated on their draft. Figure 2–7 is the value judgment and point-of-view letter of the group who prepared Figures 2–4, 2–5, and 2–6. Additional sample student point-of-view pieces, along with the graphic organizers on which they are based, are shown in Appendix 2A and Appendix 2B.

Figure 2–7. Value Judgment and Point of View of Anonymous White Female Citizen

VALUE JUDGMENT:

I like Atticus' style, like how he is patient and polite, but his willingly defending Tom Robinson! Maybe I shouldn't trust him. Mr. Gilmer's way is good because he is assertive . . . but then he comes off too strong and harsh.

REASONS:

1. Atticus really is a good man, just look at how he calls Mayella "Miss Mayella" and all. I do feel right sorry for her, coming from that family and living like they do, and now this trial. I just don't understand why he's defending that Tom Robinson.

2. The way she keeps looking around the room for answers, something seems fishy. She just went silent when Atticus started shooting off questions about what happened that day. I've never seen him treat someone that way before and it doesn't look like he's enjoying it at all. It seems like he's trying to trap her in a lie. He even says that he wants her to say something that was true about that night. I can't believe he would treat someone that way unless he really felt he had to.

3. I don't know Mr. Gilmer all that well since he's from Abbotsville, but it seems like he's pretty confident that Tom is guilty. He asks Tom questions that seem more like accusations, like he wants to make Tom out to be a liar. He even gets Tom to say that he felt sorry for Mayella! That can't be good.

4. He keeps calling Tom "boy" and Mr. Gilmer makes Tom out to look like a criminal when he asks him about the disorderly conduct charge he got for a fight. Maybe Tom isn't any different than the rest of them.

Figure 2–7. Value Judgment and Point of View of Anonymous White Female Citizen (*continued*)

Dear Connie,

I hope this letter finds you doing well. I wanted to write you about the exciting events of the past day or so. You just wouldn't believe all the fuss that is going on over here in Maycomb. I do wish you could have made it for a visit so that you could have seen the trial, but I know you have your hands full there with your family.

Now, you remember Atticus Finch? He is one of the Finches from the Landing. Comes from a real old family and he lost his wife early in their marriage. Well, he's defending a Negro against that trashy family that lives out by the county dump, the Ewells. Bob Ewell claims that Tom, the Negro man, raped his daughter. I certainly thought it could be true enough, now you know how dangerous it can be these days, but that trial has got me all confused.

I'll tell you what did it. It was the way Atticus and Mr. Gilmer, the other attorney, behaved during the trial. Atticus, as I'm sure you remember from growing up in Maycomb, treated that Mayella Ewell with the courteous respect any lady deserved. Now, she lives in filth and that daddy of hers is a drunk, but Atticus kept calling her "Miss Mayella" and saying "ma'am" to her all through the trial. I just can't for the life of me understand why he's taken Tom's side in this whole thing. You know what, though, something seems fishy about that Mayella. Atticus would ask her questions and she'd look around the room for answers. Seems like she's got something she might be hiding, but why in the world would you go through all of this trouble if it weren't true? It wasn't until the very end of his questioning of her that Atticus really seemed to lay into her.

(continues)

Figure 2–7. Value Judgment and Point of View of Anonymous White Female Citizen (*continued*)

He asked questions really fast and in a tone of voice he hadn't used all through the trial, like he was trying to prove she was lying or something. I wouldn't have wanted to be on that stand in her shoes, I'll tell you that much! I would have been scared of Atticus, yes, Atticus! It didn't seem like he wanted to do it though, treat her that way. I still just don't understand why he's gotten involved in all of this. Why somebody else couldn't have just done it is beyond me.

That Mr. Gilmer is something else. I don't know him that well, since he lives over in Abbotsville. He seemed pretty confident when he was asking that Tom Robison questions. He did him like everybody does, calling him "boy" and all that. I thought it was real interesting that Tom has a history of disorderly conduct, seems like they all can be bad if just given the chance. Mr. Gilmer, now, he even got Tom to say that he felt sorry for Mayella. Can you believe that? Tom walked right into that question without really thinking it through. Mr. Gilmer had him pretty good with that one and everyone on the jury saw it too. I guess you have to talk to them thata way and treat them like that, otherwise what will come of this place? That's just the way it is, I suppose.

Yours truly,

Sandy Mae

Summing Up

This sequence of activities includes many features of a structured process approach. During the class sessions, students do most of the work as they use graphic organizers to help them sort out points of comparison and contrast and plan and carry out their writing.

The activities scaffold students' progression through a series of increasingly complex tasks. The gateway activity is designed to draw on their knowledge of the familiar—a school-based conflict in which they may well have a vested interest. The activity, in addition to teaching narrative perspective in the context of comparison/contrast writing, contributes to students' awareness of other perspectives on issues that matter to them.

The activities rely on the collaborative development of strategies for reading carefully, thinking about perspective, and organizing and writing essays that convey students' perspectives. Students are not only "writing to learn" but "planning to learn" as they talk through their ideas. They participate in exploratory talk that produces new insights. Their initial efforts at composing are done collaboratively; they get immediate feedback that helps shape their interpretation of the differences in narrative perspective.

The emphasis throughout is on inductive learning. Not every group will develop identical procedures, but group sharing allows each group to see and discuss each other group's processes. The language lesson teaches a specific syntactic strategy that has an organic relation to the problem students are addressing.

By applying a learning strategy to a series of increasingly complex yet related tasks, students learn procedures they will be able to adapt and modify again in future tasks requiring comparing and contrasting, understanding narrative perspective, and resolving conflicting points of view. The instruction is metacognitive in that it teaches students to "learn to learn": to direct and monitor their own learning by knowing and applying procedures appropriately to tasks of a similar kind.

Appendix 2A

Organizers Leading to a Journal Entry Written
by a Childhood Friend of Tom's

Organizer 1

	MAYELLA	TOM
Similarity 1	Lives on the outside of town near the county dump/from Maycomb	Lives on the outside of town near the county dump/from Maycomb
Similarity 2	Poor	Poor
Similarity 3	Hard worker/self-respect (keeps self clean, takes care of siblings, has the geraniums she grows)	Hard worker/self-resect (works for Mr. Link Deas, offers to do work for Mayella after he's finished with work and on his way home, then does the work at his house to help his wife and kids)
Similarity 4	Looks around the courtroom for answers when given a tough question	Looks around the courtroom for answers when given a tough question
Similarity 5	Tom passed by the house a lot; on the day in question says that she invited Tom into the house; not the first time; no kids on the place	Tom passed by the house a lot; on the day in question says that he was asked to come into the house; not the first time; no kids on the place
Similarity 6	Sweating—nervous—sweaty handkerchief	Sweating—nervous—sweaty forehead
Similarity 7	Hesitates when answering; doesn't want to say the "wrong" thing (caught in lie)	Hesitates when answering; doesn't want to say the "wrong" thing (offend people)

Organizer 2

	MAYELLA	TOM
Difference 1	White female; 19 years old	Black male; married with children; 25 years old
Difference 2	Doesn't understand courtesy; offended when Atticus calls her "Miss Mayella" and "ma'am"	Is very polite, even when Mr. Gilmer uses prejudiced language toward him; understands how to be courteous and polite
Difference 3	Able bodied and strong; doesn't have a job or occupation; lives off welfare	Is handicapped due to an accident he had when he was younger; strong; works for a living as a share cropper
Difference 4	Story changes several times; hesitates each time she wants to say something different; says she never asked him inside before, but then says she has; says that she asked him to chop up a piece of furniture, she went inside to get him a nickel and that's when he jumped on her and starting beating her, knocked her out, and raped her; says she came to when she heard her father yelling; when questioned on the details, she says she can't remember	Story stays consistent; only hesitates because he doesn't want to use language that isn't okay to say in the presence of children and women; says that he chopped up the piece of furniture a long time before the day in question; says she asked him to fix a door that didn't need to be fixed and then to get something down off a chiffarobe, and when he did she jumped on him and kissed him; says he did not beat her up and the only thing disturbed was the chair he was standing on that he accidently knocked over; says he heard Mr. Ewell yelling at Mayella through the window and he ran
Difference 5	Her tone comes across as defensive	His tone is polite through the entire testimony and the cross-examination
Difference 6	Lives in a shack of a house without windows and uses the things they find at the dump to make repairs to the house/build things like fences; uses what they find at the dump to eat and live off of (tires for shoes); has no contact outside of her family (doesn't seem to know what friends are when she's asked by Atticus if she has any)	Lives in a cabin beyond the town dump, clean and well kept up, smells of food cooking when you drive by; respected member of Calpurnia's church; Mr. Link Deas stands up to defend him in the middle of the trial
Difference 7	Cries a lot on the stand, accuses Atticus of trying to take advantage of her, and refuses to answer any other questions from Atticus	Reserved on the stand, answers all of the questions he's asked to answer in a polite manner

Organizer 3

	MAYELLA	TOM
1. **status**	Poor, minimum education, lives on the outskirts of town right by the dump; isolated and alone; town isn't interested in them and she has no friends; outsider because she's a Ewell	Poor, minimum education, lives on the outskirts of town beyond the dump; outsider because of his race
2. **behavior/** **manners**	Nervous, sweaty, looks around the room for answers; impolite and cries a lot; misunderstands when people are treating her nicely; hesitates and changes her story a lot	Nervous, sweaty, looks around the room for answers; polite and honest; even when people treat him with disrespect, he's respectful; hesitates because he's worried about how the truth will be received and doesn't want to offend people
3. **testimony**	Says she asked him in to chop up a piece of furniture and that she'd pay him a nickel; says he jumped on her and started kissing her, that he beat her and the raped her; also says that she was knocked out and came to later	Says he came onto the property a number of times to help Mayella; says that on the day in question she asked him to fix a door for her inside, they went in and the door was fine; says she asked him to get something down from on top of a piece of furniture, when he did she jumped on him and asked him to kiss her; says he knocked over the chair and tried to get away from her, her dad appeared and yelled at Mayella and called her bad things and threatened her, and that was when Tom ran
4. **family/rela-** **tionships**	Oldest child and has to take care of the children; father is a drunk and hardly home; he may beat the children; he may sexually abuse Mayella; has no friends or connections in the community	Father and husband; takes care of wife and children; attends Calpurnia's church and is well respected in the Black community; Mr. Link Deas also has respect for Tom
5. **physical** **appearance**	She appears to be a strong girl who is use to doing manual labor	He appears to be strong, but he only has one good arm due to a childhood accident

Organizer 4

VALUE JUDGMENT:

Tom is clearly innocent and there is no physical way he could have done what they claim he did to Mayella; she is lying and it is clear that the Ewells just assume people will believe them because of the color of their skin.

REASONS:

1. Tom hesitates when he testifies, but it is because he doesn't want to offend anyone with the details of the incident. Mayella hesitates and changes her story every time she is pushed a little by Atticus to be clear. Her hesitation is a sign of trying to cover something up.

2. Tom is sweating and it is clear he is nervous; however, his nervousness comes from having to defend himself to the white jury and to dispute everything the Ewells have said. Mayella is sweating and nervously wadding up her handkerchief, but her nervousness seems to come from not being sure about what she's going to say. She looks around a lot at her dad and Mr. Gilmer when Atticus asks her tough questions.

3. Their stories don't match, but it is hard to believe Mayella's version simply because Tom hasn't got the use of both of his hands. In order to do all of what she says, he would need both hands to do so.

4. Tom remains respectful and polite through the testimony he gives Atticus and the cross-examination, even when Mr. Gilmer calls him terrible names and says, "boy" after every accusation. Mayella doesn't even understand that Atticus is being polite; instead she thinks he's mocking her by calling her Miss Mayella and saying "ma'am." She seems defensive, she cries, and she refuses to answer any of Atticus' questions at the end of her cross-examination. Her behavior shows she's making all of this up and believes they'll trust her simply because she's white.

5. Tom is well respected by others in the Black community; he goes to church regularly, has a nice little family, and works hard for Mr. Link Deas. Mayella doesn't seem to understand the question about friends. She is totally alone on that place and her father may physically and sexually abuse her.

I know that Tom Robinson is innocent. I've been knowing him almost my whole life. I know Tom loves his family and is a hard worker. Otherwise, why would Mr. Link Deas stand up like that in the middle of the trial? His poor wife, Helen, and those kids! What must they be goin' through right about now? I sho' hope that collection Rev. Sykes took up is helpin' them some.

It is clear he did all that outta the kindness of his heart. Doin' her chores for her and all of that. Now look, where did it get him? Defending hisself in front of all these people. He keeps as cool as he can tho'. I would be sweatin' too if I was down there on trial. He does protest just a lil' too much when Atticus asks him if he beat and raped her. That will be tough to come back from, but I understand why he's sayin' again and again. He want to be sure people know he were in the right. He stays polite and even with that ol' Mr. Gilmer callin him "boy." Just about makes me wanna crawl outta my skin when he says it like that. He says "yes, suh" and "no, suh" and that man keep on treatin' him bad.

How could he have done it? When Atticus ask that question, I was like, yeah—exactly! Everybody know that Tom got hurt when he was a lil' boy and he can't use that arm at all. How he goin' hold down a big ol' strong girl like Mayella and do all she claim he done to her? The only thing that make it look bad is that he ran. I don't blame him one bit, tho'. I'da run too. Sho' wouldn't stuck around to see whatta happen after that Mr. Ewell were there. I just hope them folks on the jury believe him. I don't know that they will, but I sho' hope they do.

She keep changin' that story of hers. Mayella don't look like she know what to say when Atticus asks her them hard questions, then she claims she can't remember. What kind of fool she take people for? She hesitates a lot before given those answers and her daddy seems like he about to jump outta his skin if she say somethin' bad about him. That cryin' fit she has may make them feel sorry for her, but who wouldn't feel sorry for her? Her life sounds terrible. Her daddy always drunk and then who knows what he may or may not do to her when he come home thata way. She sure is nervous too. That ol' handkerchief all wadded up in her hot hands. What she got to hide is what I'm thinkin'. I just hope they can see all of it and know she lyin'. Tom's life depends on it.

Appendix 2B

Organizers Leading to a Journal Entry Written by Mr. Dolphus Raymond's Wife

Organizer 1

	MAYELLA	TOM
Similarity 1	Not much money	Not much money
Similarity 2	Born and raised in Maycomb	Born and raised in Maycomb
Similarity 3	Viewed the same by citizens— low-level status	Viewed the same by citizens— low-level status
Similarity 4	Says that Tom did odd jobs	Says he did odd jobs
Similarity 5	Nervous on the stand and sweating	Nervous on the stand and sweating
Similarity 6	Not highly educated	Not highly educated
Similarity 7		

Organizer 2

	Mayella	Tom
Difference 1	White female; 19 years old	Black male; 25 years old
Difference 2	Not respectable; does not understand why people call her "ma'am" or "Miss Mayella"	Respectable; uses common manners ("yes sir," "no sir")
Difference 3	Claims that he came in and raped her	Claims that she called him in and she kissed him
Difference 4	Ewells are mean and not close (on the first day of school Burris Ewell says her daddy is "tolerable"; doesn't have any friends)	Family is close and respected (member of Calpurnia's church; Mr. Link Deas stands up and speaks in the middle of the case on behalf of Tom)
Difference 5	She is not ridiculed and is treated with respect on the stand, but is rude and disrespectful to Atticus	He is ridiculed and treated with disrespect, but remains respectful to everyone
Difference 6	She assumes people will believe her because she is white; her story changes constantly and she claims she doesn't remember when she doesn't have an answer; hesitates when answering—looks at father and Mr. Gilmer	He is afraid that people won't believe him and is unsure about telling all events/language used because of women and children that are present—only time he hesitates
Difference 7		

Organizer 3

	MAYELLA	TOM
1. status	Very poor and not much influence in Maycomb; not well educated	Poor black man, but hard worker; not well educated
2. behavior/ manners	Nervous, ignorant, insulted and hostile, no manners, hesitates because she is lying	Nervous, has manners, understands the situation he's in, hesitates because he doesn't want to offend people with what was said/ done
3. testimony	Claims that Tom beat her and raped her; goes back and forth on whether she knew him or if he'd been around before; not clear on if he had or had not been invited on the property before; says she asked him to chop up a piece of furniture	Says he didn't beat her or rape her; says he came onto the property a number of times to help and that he chopped up the piece of furniture a while back; asked to fix a door, but it wasn't broken and then she jumped on him and kissed him
4.		
5.		

Organizer 4

VALUE JUDGMENT:

Mr. Dolphus Raymond's wife can closely relate to both Tom and Mayella because of their outsider status in the community, but she would most likely side more with Tom.

REASONS:

1. They have the same social status—all are outsiders and she would be sensitive to that, but she understands what it is like to be Black in Maycomb and understands that Tom isn't sweating because he has something to hide, but because he's nervous to be up there defending himself against white people.

2. She would also understand his desire to run was not because he was guilty but because he was scared to be in the position he was in with Mayella and her father.

3. She might feel sorry for Mayella because she is lonely and has no friends and can understand what it is like to live as an outcast, but she probably wouldn't allow that to be an excuse for her claims that Tom raped her. Mayella's hesitation on the stand and her treatment of Atticus would keep Mr. Raymond's wife from believing her story or respecting her.

4. The physical evidence that Tom wouldn't be able to beat her up and rape her because of his disability would also hurt Mayella's claims; the fact that her father is left-handed and because Mayella at first said her father beat her when he was drunk but then hesitated and changed her story only after making eye contact with him would lead Mrs. Raymond to believe that Mr. Ewell may have beat her up that day.

5. Tom's ability to stay respectful and polite through the entire testimony and cross-examination even when Mr. Gilmer calls him "boy" could convince Mrs. Raymond that he's a good person; the fact that he helped Mayella often after work because she looked like she needed the help would also show his helpful nature; Mayella's family doesn't do anything to help others or themselves—father is a drunk that lives off welfare, he may possibly beat and sexually abuse his children, they live in filth, and she doesn't understand common courtesy of being called "miss" and "ma'am."

I sat there today in that courtroom and it was all hot and crowded. Stuffy like there was no air. Everybody hanging on every word from Tom and Mayella's mouths. Didn't seem like anyone was hardly breathing, they were all so lost in the details of their testimony. Even the babies were quiet! I watched those lawyers go back and forth and back and forth. It didn't seem like it would end. I listed to her words, Mayella's words, closely. She claims he raped her, but that's not Tom, not to mention the fact that it would be awfully hard to do considering his arm. I feel sorry for her, I really do. Just look at how she behaves to being called "Miss Mayella" and "ma'am." She's never been treated that way by these people before, why wouldn't she think they were just mocking her or trying to take advantage? She seems so alone and she's so young. She's raising all of those brothers and sisters of hers all alone. That no good daddy of theirs just drinks up what money they do get and then he beats them, possibly sexually abuses her! She keeps looking at him for answers, like she's afraid to tell the truth. I just can't imagine. It must be hard for them to get by. Maybe this is her way to scream out for attention, but I just don't understand why she has to try and do it by hurting someone else. There is a part of me that understands her loneliness and her wanting to be a part of things. They look at them like they look at us. Part of me wants to believe her. What if she is telling the truth? But then, I know better. Look at Tom. He's polite and kind, even when Mr. Gilmer says those nasty things to him and talks to him like he's no good. Mr. Deas seems to think Tom is a good person, otherwise why would he risk standing up like that in front of everyone and saying so. I just wish he'd taken the stand to defend Tom, but he's just scared. Scared of what this place would think of him. Why else would he do all of those things for her unless he was a kind person? It wasn't like he was getting anything in return and then he had to go home and help Helen. People in this town have no idea what it is like to live like an outcast. To be casted off like trash. I know. I know that Mayella knows. I think that's why Tom reached out to her like he did 'cause he knows it too. But they won't let him get off. That's for sure. He is Black and they can't have a Black man winning, especially against a white woman's words, even if that woman is treated like trash. So this is just going to end up like the others, right? It is just a real shame.

3

What Makes This a Structured Process Approach?

As we hope we have demonstrated in the pages of this book, we believe that kids learn best when actively engaged in activities that interest them. This premise is the foundation of a structured process approach. Now that you have seen what teaching this way looks like, we'll lay out the basic principles that guided our planning and that might guide yours, too, going forward:

- The teacher usually identifies the task, such as writing a comparison/contrast essay, although students may participate in deciding what they want to learn how to write. Even with the task identified, students often begin learning the processes involved by participating in simple activities such as comparing and contrasting two local radio stations.

- Learning begins with *activity* rather than with the product of that learning. For example, when comparing radio stations, students brainstorm a list of similarities and differences and then prioritize their importance.

- The teacher designs and sequences activities that allow students to move through increasingly challenging problems of the same type. For example, in Chapter 1, after comparing and contrasting familiar things like local radio stations, students research and compare/contrast two nationally known singing groups.

- Students' learning is highly social, involving continual talk with one another as they learn procedures and strategies for particular kinds of writing. In the lessons in this book, small groups of students discuss similarities and differences, decide which ones to include in their essay and how to present them, and co-construct a draft.

- The teacher designs the activities that take students through the particular writing process that produces the final product. However, in class, *the students are the ones talking and doing.* The teacher's role is primarily to help students apply the strategies, not to exercise a heavy hand in leading discussions and guiding the writing.

A structured process approach therefore places the teacher in the role of designer and orchestrator of student activity through which the *students themselves* make many of the decisions about how to write and how to assess the quality of their writing. Figure 3–1 is a

Figure 3–1. Principles of a Structured Process Approach

1. Instruction allows students to develop procedures for how to compose in relation to particular kinds of tasks. The processes that students use to write comparison/contrast essays, for example, are different from those used to write personal narratives.

2. Because different tasks require different procedures, writing instruction cannot rely solely on general strategies. Rather than simply learning "prewriting" as an all-purpose strategy, students learn how to prewrite in connection with a specific genre—writing a comparison/contrast essay, for example, in which case small groups of students might explore the similarities and differences between particular people, places, or things and write about them informally.

(continues)

Figure 3–1. Principles of a Structured Process Approach (*continued*)

3. With writing instruction focused on specific tasks, students work toward clear and specific goals with a particular community of readers in mind. An essay advocating one brand of cell phone over another might be addressed to a parent about to purchase one for the student, to a general readership of teenagers in a product review, or to a corporation recommending that they improve their phone. Each readership expects different rhetorical features and responds differently to interpersonal issues.

4. Even with clear and specific goals, thinking and writing are open-ended. Essay content, structure, diction, and other elements vary from writer to writer, depending on one's knowledge, the nature of the entities being compared, and one's audience. Students operating from different assumptions could take opposing perspectives in choosing between one restaurant's French fries over another's, one Heisman Trophy candidate's merits for the award relative to others, one pancake recipe's leavening agents over another, and so on.

5. Composing is a highly social act, rather than the work of an individual. Students discuss their compositions with peers at every stage of development. In a structured process approach, people learn to write by *talking* as well as by writing.

6. The teacher and students share an understanding of the criteria used to assess the writing. Students often help develop these evaluative criteria by discussing what they value in the writing they read. When the writing is tied to large-scale assessment, such as writing a comparison/contrast essay for a district or state gateway exam, the criteria may already be in place.

7. The teacher *scaffolds* students' learning of procedures by designing activities and providing materials that the students may manipulate. Initial instruction is simple and

Figure 3–1. Principles of a Structured Process Approach (*continued*)

manageable. For example, when learning how to write comparison/contrast essays, students might first explore familiar material through informal writing. Instruction then progresses through more challenging aspects of the writing, such as persuading particular audiences or responding to challenges posed by readers. Attention to form comes later in the instruction when students have developed content to write about, rather than earlier, as is often the case with instruction in how to write the five-paragraph theme and other forms.

8. When possible, the teacher provides additional readerships for students' writing, such as having the students post their writing in the classroom or on a classroom wiki or submit their writing to a contest, the school newspaper, the school literary magazine, and so on.

more comprehensive list of principles that guide this approach. We and other teachers influenced by George Hillocks have outlined this approach in a number of publications, including Hillocks (1975, 2006), Hillocks, McCabe, and McCampbell (1971), Johannessen, Kahn, and Walter (1982, 2009), Kahn, Walter, and Johannessen (1984), Lee (1993), McCann, Johannessen, Kahn, Smagorinsky, and Smith (2005), Smagorinsky (2008), and Smagorinsky, McCann, and Kern (1987). Several of these titles are available for free download at www.coe .uga.edu/~smago/Books/Free_Downloadable_Books.htm.

Designing Structured Process Instruction

A structured process approach to teaching writing involves two key ideas: *environmental teaching* and *inquiry instruction* (Hillocks 1995).

Environmental Teaching

One important assumption that underlies environmental teaching is the belief that *each task we ask students to do involves unique ways of thinking.* By way of example, think of what is involved in three types of writing tasks: defining effective leadership, comparing and contrasting two leaders, and writing a personal narrative about providing leadership. Each relies on different ways of thinking and communicating one's thinking in writing, and each involves different rhetorical features. An environmental approach, then, stresses learning particular sets of *procedures* for engaging in specific sorts of *tasks* so as to produce a *form* that meets the expectations of readers.

To help students learn to accomplish a new task, a teacher needs to involve students directly in developing strategies for undertaking that task. In other words, the teacher introduces activities that will help students learn *how* to do this new kind of thinking and writing.

A task in this sense involves both *doing* something and *thinking about how it's done* so that it can be done again with different materials. A task, then, may comprise writing a personal narrative, or comparing and contrasting similar yet different things, or arguing in favor of a solution, or defining a complex concept such as progress or success. Our goal for students is that when they complete this task, they are able to repeat the process more independently next time by applying their procedural and strategic knowledge to new material.

Inquiry Instruction

Inquiry is the particular structure through which students work, often in collaboration with one another.

Again, the teacher plays a strong role designing activities that provide the basis for students' inquiries into the problems they investigate. For comparison/contrast essays, the problem may be *how* to compare and contrast two similar yet distinct things.

The students play with materials related to the questions they hope to settle through their writing. *Play* in this sense refers to experimenting with ideas, and while it may involve a great deal of fun, may also be quite serious. Let's say students need to develop categories by which to compare and contrast two things, such as soccer players they admire, the food at different restaurants with similar menus, or the merits of a pair of novelists such as Judy Blume and Jacqueline Woodson. To help them, the teacher might have students, in small groups, discuss two items informally, encouraging them to experiment with *what if?* questions and other explorations that help them clarify their views. In one recent discussion of this kind, a group comparing and contrasting two popular brands of cell phones discussed their comparative merits as to ease of keyboard use, quality of reception, availability of apps (applications), readability of interface, and so on. They then ranked these categories according to importance, evaluated the differences between the two cell phones, and ultimately determined which phone was preferable.

Students' work is open-ended in that the activities may have many plausible solutions or outcomes. One person might choose one phone over the other by ordering the features to establish their importance; another might determine ease of use according to idiosyncratic preferences. Small-group discussions allow students to play with these ideas to try out solutions that may or may not ultimately figure into the final decision.

Applying Structured Process Instruction

This book illustrates how you might put these principles into practice when teaching students to write comparison/contrast essays. By deliberately working through the various stages required to complete an immediate product, your students have an opportunity to write essays that matter to them and that gradually improve in quality. The process of producing these essays contributes to their understanding of their experiences. With their explicit knowledge of thinking and writing procedures, they will be able to apply them to other situations involving comparison/contrast when they work independently. Students address a particular problem, work with specific problem-solving strategies, and rehearse their writing in discussions with other students before they put their ideas on paper.

What Can You Expect When Teaching Writing with This Approach?

Preparing students to write well-developed, thoughtful comparison/contrast essays is time-consuming for both you and your students. The detailed, systematic process outlined in this book sequences students' progress through procedures for both thinking about and writing a comparison/contrast essay. The activities cannot attend to *all* the considerations in completing a task this complicated and interactive, and often other curricular imperatives limit the time available to teach any ability thoroughly and effectively. Realistically, before students are able to apply specific skills and strategies to new situations, they will need several experiences and appropriate feedback from you, from other students, and if possible from other readers. However, with continual reinforcement, the procedures that students generate should enable them to write strong comparison/contrast essays on future occasions when they choose or are called upon to create them.

Where Do You Go from Here?

This book and the others in this series provide specific plans you can adapt to your own teaching. They also introduce you to a process you can use to design original instruction based on your classroom and your students' needs. The guide below will help you design writing instruction using a structured process approach:

1. *Identify the task that will form the basis for your instruction.* Assuming that any general process such as "prewriting" differs depending on the demands of particular writing tasks, identify the task that will form the basis of the instruction. This task might be specified by a formal writing requirement and assessment provided by a mandate from the school, district, or state (e.g., argumentation); it might be writing that you believe is essential in your students' education (e.g., research reports); it might be writing that students identify as something they want to learn how to do (e.g., college application essays); or it might come from some other source or inspiration.

2. *Conduct an inventory of students' present writing qualities and needs.* With the task identified, you will probably want to see what students' writing of this sort looks like prior to instruction. Doing so allows you to focus on students' needs and avoid teaching strategies they already know.

3. *Conduct a task analysis.* Either by consulting existing sources or by going through the processes involved in carrying out the writing task yourself, identify what students need to know in order to write effectively according to the demands of readers. The task analysis should treat both *form* (e.g., using conjunctive adverbs to highlight comparisons and contrast within sentences) and *procedure* (e.g., how to determine the relative importance of comparison/contrast categories). The task analysis will also help you identify the evaluative criteria that you ultimately use to assess student work.

4. *Conduct an activity analysis.* Determine the types of activities that will engage students with materials that are likely to foster their understanding of the processes involved in the task. Identify familiar and accessible materials (e.g., local radio stations or restaurants) for the early stages of their learning, and introduce more complex concepts (e.g., comparison of works of literature) for subsequent activities.

5. *Design and sequence students' learning experiences so that they provide a scaffold.* Design increasingly challenging tasks of the same sort using increasingly complex materials. Sequence these activities so that students are always reiterating the process but doing so in the face of greater challenges. The activities should present continual opportunities for students to talk with one another as they learn the processes involved in carrying out the task.

6. *Consider opportunities to teach language usage in the context of learning procedures for task-related writing.* Specific kinds of writing often benefit from particular language strategies. For example, students need to learn how to introduce points of similarity and difference smoothly and fluidly. Targeting language instruction to specific instances of its use helps overcome the problem inherent in discrete grammar instruction, which is that it fails to improve students' understanding of how to speak and write clearly.

7. *Relying on the task analysis, develop rubrics through which students clearly understand the expectations for their writing.* These rubrics may be developed in consultation with students, adopted from established criteria such as those provided for state writing tests or advanced placement exams, adopted from model rubrics available on the Internet, created by examining a set of student work that represents a range of performance, and so on.

8. *Provide many opportunities during the learning process for feedback and revision.* Students should be given many occasions to get feedback on drafts of their writing. This feedback can come by way of peer response groups, your written response to their writing, writing conferences with you, or other means.

A Structured Process Approach and Professional Learning Communities

Currently many school faculties constitute a professional learning community made up of collaborative teams. Structured process instruction is particularly effective in this context. Teachers together develop instruction and analyze student work. Teams use the student writing produced during the instructional sequence as a basis for discussing what worked, what students are struggling with, and what should be done differently or what needs to be added. They collaboratively design rubrics for scoring student work so that expectations for students are consistent. Collecting data on student performance from pretest to final product allows the group to evaluate student growth, reflect on the strengths and weaknesses of the instruction, and plan future classroom activities.

Our own teaching has shown us that this approach can greatly improve students' writing over the course of instruction. We look forward to hearing how you have adopted this approach to your own teaching and helped your students learn how to use written expression to meet their responsibilities as students, writers, friends, communicators, and citizens.

References

Applebee, A. N. 1996. *Curriculum as Conversation: Transforming Traditions of Teaching and Learning.* Chicago: University of Chicago Press.

Dale, H. 1994. "Collaborative Research on Collaborative Writing." *English Journal* 83(1): 66–70.

Hillocks, G. 1975. *Observing and Writing.* Urbana, IL: National Council of Teachers of English. Retrieved December 6, 2008 from www.coe.uga.edu/~smago/Books/Observing_and _Writing.pdf.

———. 1986. *Research on Written Composition: New Directions for Teaching.* Urbana, IL: National Conference on Research in English and Educational Resources Information Center.

———. 1995. *Teaching Writing as Reflective Practice.* New York: Teachers College Press.

———. 2002. *The Testing Trap: How State Writing Assessments Control Learning.* New York: Teachers College Press.

———. 2006. *Narrative Writing: Learning a New Model for Teaching.* Portsmouth, NH: Heinemann.

Hillocks, G. Jr., E. Kahn, and L. Johannessen. 1983. "Teaching Defining Strategies as a Mode of Inquiry." *Research in the Teaching of English* 17: 275–84.

Hillocks, G., B. McCabe, and J. McCampbell. 1971. *The Dynamics of English Instruction, Grades 7–12.* New York: Random House. Retrieved August 4, 2006 from www.coe.uga.edu/~smago /Books/Dynamics/Dynamics_home.htm.

Johannessen, L. R., E. Kahn, and C. C. Walter. 1982. *Designing and Sequencing Prewriting Activities.* Urbana, IL: National Council of Teachers of English. Retrieved July 2, 2008 from www.coe.uga .edu/~smago/Books/Designing_and_Sequencing.pdf.

———. 2009. *Writing About Literature*. 2d ed. Urbana, IL: National Council of Teachers of English.

Kahn, E., C. Walter, and L. R. Johannessen. 1984. *Writing About Literature*. Urbana, IL: National Council of Teachers of English.

Lee, C. D. 1993. *Signifying as a Scaffold for Literary Interpretation: The Pedagogical Implications of an African American Discourse Genre*. Urbana, IL: National Council of Teachers of English.

Marshall, J. D., P. Smagorinsky, and M. W. Smith. 1995. *The Language of Interpretation: Patterns of Discourse in Discussions of Literature*. NCTE Research Report No. 27. Urbana, IL: National Council of Teachers of English.

McCann, T. M., L. R. Johannessen, E. Kahn, P. Smagorinsky, and M. W. Smith, eds. 2005. *Reflective Teaching, Reflective Learning: How to Develop Critically Engaged Readers, Writers, and Speakers*. Portsmouth, NH: Heinemann.

Nelson, J., and J. R. Hayes. 1988. *How the Writing Context Shapes College Students' Writing Strategies for Writing from Sources*. Center for the Study of Writing, Technical Report No. 16. Berkeley, CA, and Pittsburgh, PA: University of California–Berkeley and Carnegie-Mellon University. ED 297374.

Nystrand, M. 1997. *Opening Dialogue: Understanding the Dynamics of Language and Learning in the English Classroom*. New York: Teachers College Press.

Smagorinsky, P. 1991. "The Writer's Knowledge and the Writing Process: A Protocol Analysis." *Research in the Teaching of English* 25: 339–64.

———. 2008. *Teaching English by Design: How to Create and Carry Out Instructional Units*. Portsmouth, NH: Heinemann.

Smagorinsky, P., T. McCann, and S. Kern. 1987. *Explorations: Introductory Activities for Literature and Composition, Grades 7–12*. Urbana, IL: National Council of Teachers of English. Retrieved December 8, 2008 from www.coe.uga.edu/~smago/Books /Explorations.pdf.

Smith, M. W. 1989. "Teaching the Interpretation of Irony in Poetry." *Research in the Teaching of English* 23: 254–72.

Weaver, C. 1996. *Teaching Grammar in Context*. Portsmouth, NH: Heinemann.

Teaching Students to Write

The Dynamics of Writing Instruction series

- ▶ **Argument**
- ▶ **Essays That Define**
- ▶ **Comparison/Contrast Essays**
- ▶ **Personal Narratives**
- ▶ **Research Reports**
- ▶ **Fictional Narratives**

Designed to provide teachers with resources that ensure students gain the writing skills needed for success in college and careers

"These books will support teachers in their understanding of designing process-based instruction and give them both useful lesson plans and a process for designing instruction on their own that follows the design principles."

—Peter Smagorinsky, Larry Johannessen,
Elizabeth Kahn, and Thomas McCann

Argument / Grades 6–12 / 978-0-325-03400-3 / 2011 / 96pp est. / $14.50
Essays That Define / Grades 6–12 / 978-0-325-03401-0 / 2011 / 96pp est. / $14.50
Comparison/Contrast Essays / Grades 6–12 / 978-0-325-03398-3 / Spring 2012 / 96pp est. / $14.50
Personal Narratives / Grades 6–12 / 978-0-325-03397-6 / Spring 2012 / 96pp est. / $14.50
Research Reports / Grades 6–12 / 978-0-325-03402-7 / Spring 2012 / 96pp est. / $14.50
Fictional Narratives / Grades 6–12 / 978-0-325-03399-0 / Spring 2012 / 96pp est. / $14.50

CALL **800.225.5800**   WEB **Heinemann.com**   FAX **877.231.6980**   DEDICATED TO TEACHERS

Franklin Pierce University

00199418

DATE DUE

PRINTED IN U.S.A.